Blueprint for a Crooked House

BLUEPRINT FOR A CROOKED HOUSE

Reflective Analysis and Synthesis of the Factors that Caused the Collapse of a $10 billion Global Joint Venture between AT&T and British Telecom: A Case Study

Blueprint for a Crooked House

Copyright © 2005 Jidé Odubiyi

ISBN 0-9770191-1-X

All rights reserved. No part of this publication may be reproduced, stored in a retrieval system, or transmitted in any form or by any means, electronic, mechanical, recording or otherwise, without the prior written permission of the author.

Library of Congress Control Number: 2005908506

Printed in the United States of America.

SEGMA BOOKS
An imprint of ILORI Press Books LLC
13217 New Hampshire Avenue, #10332
Silver Spring, MD 20904

Cover and layout © ILORI Press Books
Cover photo © Dusit Panyakhom/123rf

BLUEPRINT FOR A CROOKED HOUSE

Reflective Analysis and Synthesis of the Factors that Caused the Collapse of a $10 billion Global Joint Venture between AT&T and British Telecom: A Case Study

Jidé B. Odubiyi, Ph.D.

SEGMA BOOKS
Silver Spring, Maryland

Blueprint for a Crooked House

Dedication

This book is dedicated to the memory of Dr. George Lermer a former faculty member in the School of Management of Walden University, who died in a skiing accident on March 15, 2003. He was 62. As one of the reviewers of this case study research, he provided me with excellent guidance resulting in the successful completion of this study.

Blueprint for a Crooked House

Acknowledgements

I would like to thank Daniel Moorhead, Director of Organizational Research, BT Group North America for sharing his experience and insights on merger risks, merger failure rates, and his research results from learning histories on MCI-BT merger failure. Thanks to Janis Ackerman, former Business Manager of Concert for explaining management rationale for certain decisions made by company management. I am also grateful to Jamil Khan of Concert for allowing me to reference his research results on the decline of the telecom industry with special reference to Concert to validate this study. Thanks to Dr. Robin Schaller of Walden University for his constructive comments as a reviewer of this study. Finally, I am very thankful to my wife Marion, and my daughter Folasade, for their selfless support, honest input, and review of the final manuscript.

Blueprint for a Crooked House

Blueprint for a Crooked House

TABLE OF CONTENTS

ABSTRACT 1

INTRODUCTION 3

Differences in Development of Mergers/Acquisitions and Joint Ventures 5

CHAPTER 1: HISTORY OF CONCERT 9

Background 9

Prior Merger Experiences of this Author, BT, and AT&T 13

Background on BT and AT&T 13
    Some Lessons Learned from the Failure of MCI-BT Merger 14

Concert Business Story and its Activation as a Global Joint Venture 16

Motivations, Purpose and Significance of this Study 17
    Purpose of the Study 19
    Significance of the Study 19

Summary 20

CHAPTER 2: STUDY ASSUMPTIONS, RATIONALE FOR SELECTING THE CASE STUDY APPROACH, AND ORGANIZATIONAL THEORIES 21

Assumptions and Limitations of the Study 21

Case Study Research 23
    Data Collection and Analysis in Case Study Research 25
    Research Challenges in Case Study Research 25

Assumptions on the Cultural Aspects of this Study 26

Viewing Organizations as Complex and Open Systems 26
    The Issue of Organizational Control 29

Organizational Control Issues for Complex Organizations 30

Summary 30

CHAPTER 3: SOCIO-TECHNICAL SYSTEMS THEORY AND ORGANIZATIONS 31

Socio-technical Systems Theory 31
    Background on Socio-technical Systems 31
    Development of Socio-technical Systems Theory 32

Organizations as Socio-technical Systems 33

Organizational Systems: Balancing the Technical, Social, and Environmental for Survival 34
    The Technical Perspective of the Organization 36
    The Social Perspective of an Organization 37

Designing Socio-technical Systems 38

Summary 40

CHAPTER 4: LEADERSHIP, ORGANIZATIONAL CHANGE MANAGEMENT THEORIES, AND TRIANGULATION PROTOCOLS 41

Organizational Leadership Issues and Change Management in Mergers and Acquisitions 41
    Managing Three Levels of Organizational Change with STS 42
    Empowerment 45

In Search of a Working Leadership Model for Organizational Change Management 46
    Leadership Perspectives 48

Normative View of Organizational Leadership 48
Internal Integration and External Adaptation 49
Leadership Development 51

Leadership and Organizational Change Management 54
Leaders' Difficulties with Change 54
Change as a Demanding Process 56
Six Barriers to Organizational Change 57
Leadership in Practice 58

Triangulation Protocols for Validating the Results of this Study .. 60
A Brief Review of Triangulation Protocols 61

Summary 61

CHAPTER 5: ANALYSIS OF CONCERT'S ORGANIZATIONAL DEVELOPMENT PROCESS 62

Compliance with the Phases of STS Design and Leadership Models 62
Concert STS Discovery Process 63
Organizational System Understanding Process 65
Organizational System Design Phase: Design for the Ideal Organization 65
Implementation of Concert STS Process 67

Concert Leadership Model 69

Concert Performance Management Principles 70
Four Phases of Concert Performance Management Activity 71
Tabular Summaries of Concert Leadership Model 75
Concert Employee Annual Survey 80
Concert Employee Survey Related to Concert Leadership Model— Culture Dimension 81
Responses to Open-ended Question Themes: Aspects of Company Valued Most/Valued Least 85

Summary 85

CHAPTER 6: EVALUATION OF THE PROBLEMS OF CONCERT GLOBAL JOINT VENTURE AND SUGGESTED SOLUTIONS 86

Problems of the Joint Venture and Suggested Solutions 86
- Clash of Leadership Cultures 86
- Absence of Trust between the Partners 90
- Imbalance Structure of the New Organization 90
- Open Competition Between Subsidiaries 91
- Over Investment in Telecommunication Infrastructure 91
- Dream of Initial Public Offering 91
- Lukewarm Embrace of Organizational Learning 92
- Additional Problems of the Global Joint Venture 93

Evaluation of the Operations of the Global Joint Venture from STS Perspectives 93
- Successful Applications of the STS Process 94
- Weaknesses in the Implementation of the STS Process 94

Comparison of data on Concert Leadership Model against Successful Leadership Practices 95
- Effectiveness of Concert Leadership Model 95
- Comparing the Concert Alliance Process against the "Seven Deadly Sins of Mergers" 97

Validation of Data on Causes of the Failure of the Joint Venture 102
- Data Source Triangulation 103
- Investigator Triangulation 103
- The Importance of Communication and Cultural Understanding Between Partners 108
- English versus English—Separated by a Common Language (Winston Churchill) 109

Evaluating the Collapse of Concert from a Risk Management Perspective 110
- Risk Dimension #1: Structural Complexity of Concert (low or high) 110
- Risk Dimension #2: Dynamic Complexity of Industry (stable or turbulent) 110
- Risk Dimension #3: Partner Compatibility—corporate cultures (common or divergent profile) 111

Risk Dimension #4: Partner Compatibility (strong or weak mutual trust) 112
Risk Dimension #5: Alignment of Goals and Principles (compatible or divergent) 112
Risk Dimension #6: Alignment Dynamics – Handling Alliance Conflict (Collaborative or Adversarial) 113

Summary 113

CHAPTER 7: CONCLUSION 115

REFERENCES 117

APPENDIX A. CULTURAL ISSUES: TWO NATIONS (UK AND US) DIVIDED BY A COMMON LANGUAGE 124

APPENDIX B. PROFILES AND HISTORICAL SHARE PRICES OF AT&T, BT, AND MCI 132

APPENDIX C. LIST OF ACRONYMS 133

INDEX 134

ABOUT THE AUTHOR 149

Blueprint for a Crooked House

LIST OF TABLES

Table 2-1: Quantitative and Qualitative Assumptions............................22

Table 2-2: Rationale for Selecting a Research Paradigm........................23

Table 2-3: Dimension of Organizational Operational Context....................27

Table 2-4: Understanding Organizational Control Issues 29

Table 3-1: Comparison of the Socio-technical Model with the Traditional Model 39

Table 4-1: Dimensions of Successful Change Management 44

Table 4-2: Empowerment: Choosing Centralization or Decentralization 45

Table 5-1: Concert Leadership Model—Customer Cultural Dimension... ...76

Table 5-2: Concert Leadership Model—Collaboration 77

Table 5-3: Concert Leadership Model—Creativity 78

Table 5-4: Concert Leadership Model—Results 79

Table 5-5: Open-ended Survey Questions: Valued Most and Valued Least..84

Table 6-1: American Consumer (Post-Merger) Satisfaction Index 101

Blueprint for a Crooked House

LIST OF FIGURES

Figure 1-1: A global telecommunication network of Concert 9

Figure 1-2: Telecom Operations Map (TOM): business process framework..12

Figure 3-1. An Organization as a Socio-Technical System (STS) 35

Figure 5-1: A Roadmap of the Socio-technical system mapped to Concert development process 62

Blueprint for a Crooked House

ABSTRACT

This case study presents a reflective analysis of the factors that caused the failure of a $10 billion global joint venture between AT&T and British Telecom. The global joint venture, named Concert, closed its doors after 2 ½ years of operation in June 2002.

This study describes Concert Global Networks, a telecommunication service provider that provided global telecommunication services to multi-national companies. Concert is (defined as) a complex organization. The structure of the organization and how that structure fits into the framework of a socio-technical system theory is assessed and described. This study also presents an evaluation of Concert leadership model and analysis of the results of an annual survey of employees. A major conclusion of this study is that the failure of Concert was due to implementation failure brought about by the inability of the leadership to manage risks relating to divergent goals of the partners, divergent corporate cultures, weak mutual trust between partners, inefficient customer service, lukewarm support of organizational learning, and alliance conflict. In addition, Concert had a flawed business model. The model relied on distributors' networks, over which it had no control, to deliver its telecommunication services to its customers while it was responsible for guaranteeing delivery of the services. The leadership team did not identify the flaw in the business model until several months after the start of operations.

The failure to identify the flaw in the business model could be attributed to the failure to integrate the two managerial cultures. This case study also reports the significant drain on the global economy by failures of joint ventures. A conservative estimate places the failure rate of joint ventures at 60-80 percent at a cost of several hundred billion dollars annually. This study presents results from multiple sources that show that losses, from organizations that have gone through mergers and acquisitions, outweigh any reported profits. What is supported by research is that the buyer often pays too much. The seller benefits while the buyer does not, but the merger itself often creates value because the gain to the seller exceeds the loss to the loser. While the decline of demand and major oversupply of communication services contributed to the downfall of Concert, there were significant structural, management, and operational factors that exacerbated the problems. These factors (analyzed, synthesized, and reported in this book) in the view of this author constitute a blueprint for a crooked house.

*"**Those who cannot remember the past are condemned to repeat it.**"*
George Santayana (1863-1952), The Life of Reason, vol. I
Reason in Common Sense.

INTRODUCTION

Case study research involves studying a phenomenon bounded by time and activity-such as an event, a process, or a program, and collecting detailed information with different collection methods for an extended time period (Creswell, 1994). In this case study, I analyze and report my in depth investigation of a specific business phenomenon-the collapse of a $10 billion global joint venture Concert Global Networks Inc. (hereafter called Concert) between the American Telephone & Telegraph Corp. (AT&T) and British Telecommunications private limited company (BTplc). The parties to the joint venture established Concert to provide telecommunication services to multinational corporations (i.e., companies with branches in several countries).

The motivation for this case study is that Concert was a failure. It is not unique. Failure is common in joint ventures, mergers and acquisitions (Grinblatt & Titman, 2002; Knowles-Cutler & Bradbury, 2002; Martin, 2001; and Skapinker, 2000). Many researchers and practitioners argue that failures are a result of weakness in the implementation of the process of integrating personnel with different cultures into a new corporate community (Marks & Mirvis, 1998; Harari, 1999; Martin, 2001; Moorhead, 1998a; and Schein, 1996). The same view is shared by White and McCarthy (2004) in reporting on the Sprint-Nextel merger asserting that the "merger would require the meshing of two companies that have different cultures, technologies, and reputation" (White & McCarthy, 2004). A variety of factors contributed to Concert's failure. Chief among these was weak implementation of the integration process. This case study is a diagnosis of Concert's failure to integrate its two constituent members. That diagnosis identifies several considerations that future managers of joint ventures should carefully consider to improve the chances of a successful integration of the partners to the venture and a successful economic outcome.

The study covers a critical period of three years— from 1998 when the intent to form Concert was first announced through 2001, when the decision was made to dissolve the joint venture. Concert ceased to exist in June 2002.

The data presented and analyzed in this study were collected over the life of the joint venture. At the time this author worked as a manager for the Research and Development section of British Telecom North America (BTNA), a firm that was merged into the joint venture.

As mentioned earlier, failure of Concert is not unique. According to Skapinker, 65 percent of all mergers and acquisitions fail (Skapinker, 2000). During the first quarter of 2000, $1,166 billion dollars were invested globally on mergers and acquisitions. On the jacket of their book—*Joining Forces*, Marks and Mirvis (1998) report that 75 percent of all mergers and acquisitions fail. They based their conclusion on their involvement in 50 mergers over a fifteen-year period while they served as organizational researchers and consultants to very large corporations. Marks and Mirvis consider successful mergers as mergers that position the new company to build core competencies, gain new technologies, penetrate new markets, and achieve significant growth. They consider successfully managed alliances as those characterized by consolidated strengths of the two entities that achieve their business objectives through successful transition and productive synthesis of four business areas[1]—strategy, organization, culture, and people to make the new organization more productive than the separate companies. (Marks & Mirvis, 1998, p. 275). In my view, just as successful marriages are not measured by the family income alone, the same should be true for successful alliances. Successful alliances are those positioned to survive. If an organization is positioned to survive, financial success can be assured. Failed mergers are mergers that cannot adapt to the pressures inherent in the new relationship.

In affirming that while 65 percent of mergers fail, Skapinker concludes that 35 percent of them succeed. He then describes what success means. Citing the opinion of Ken Favaro, a managing partner of Marakon in the United Kingdom, with experience working for Boeing,

---

[1] Strategy involves managing the new organization with constant focus on its strategic objectives to build a new and better organization. There should also be a focus on the human element, develop a desired culture from a combination of the two cultures.

Coca-Cola, and Lloyds TSB, he identifies two conditions for success. The first condition provides the situation where the shareholders' returns on their investments in the combined company, are higher than combined returns from the two companies managed as separate entities. While this is a good definition, it is not that easy to apply because the shareholder's required rate of return rises and falls with the market. A more accurate definition would be that the shareholders' returns on their investments in the combined company are higher several years after the merger than the combined returns from the two companies managed as separate entities would have been (Thornton, 2004). The latter is a *counterfactual* – and has to be determined during the Capital Asset Pricing Model to forecast what the separate share prices would have been if the companies had remained independent.

Secondly, the two entities' ability to identify which partner's process will be employed in the combined company, and the managers' ability to determine the strategic benefits that the new company would bring that will be difficult for competitors to copy.

Differences in Development of Mergers/Acquisitions and Joint Ventures

The development process for mergers and acquisitions (M&A) are different from joint ventures. A merger or acquisition may be prompted when one management team, believing it can increase the value of the assets currently managed by another team or the merger, may flow from confidence that there are synergies to be tapped in combining the two firms.

A joint venture (JV) is a more limited organizational model in which two independent management teams see an opportunity to serve a market niche at a lower cost or more effectively in partnership with a second firm. The partners set up the joint venture management. The joint venture is not necessarily a means of one management team displacing another, as is typically the case in a merger or acquisition. Although there are differences in the approach used to form M&A versus JV. The new entities in both approaches face very similar problems, possibly on a smaller scale with JVs. At the same time the criteria for success are identical. Consequently, lessons learned from this study that focuses on a JV can benefit managers of M&As.

Grinblatt and Titman (2002) report empirical studies that show that from the early 1960s to the mid-1970s and even through 1980s, diversifications were profitable. During this period cash-starved firms were eager to merge with cash-rich firms to reduce financial risks of introducing new products. According to research reported by Comment and Jarrell in 1995 (cited in Grinblatt and Titman, 2002, p. 710) the value of corporations decrease when they diversify and increase when they sell off divisions to focus on their core businesses. The average return during the 1970s was stated as 1.31 percent and in the 1980s the average return was 6.97 percent. The result of a study of accounting data of over 500 mergers between 1950 and 1975 conducted by Ravenscraft and Scherer found significant decrease in profitability of the acquired firms after the merger. (Cited in Grinblatt and Titman, 2002, p. 711). The result of a study of approximately 2000 mergers during 1973 to 1998 conducted by Andrade, Mitchell, and Stafford in 2001 suggests that subsequent to the merger both firms showed about 1 percent profit. There is a large body of literature on mergers and acquisitions. One could follow the wealth transfer paradigm that buyers tend to overpay and sellers are better off than buyers. The loss accrues for the shareholders of takeover firms, but that loss is offset by a gain to the shareholders of the selling firm. While the evidence from Ravenscaft and Scherer's study does not support this view, the challenge is the validity of the accounting process. The problems with the accounting practices of large companies such as, Enron, Arthur Anderson, Adelphia Communications, and WorldCom; and the deceptive practices of brokerage houses on Wall Street make it very difficult to reach any valid conclusion.

Lessons learned from this study can help reduce the amount of loss incurred by companies through mergers and acquisitions. Daniel Moorhead, the Director of Organizational Research, BT Group North America (one of the experts consulted for this study) reports in a learning history document that he developed following the failure of a previous merger attempt between MCI and BT that the average failure rate for all mergers is about 75 percent (Moorhead, 1998) and that mergers result in a significant drain on the global economy. His report is based on Marks and Mirvis (1998) cited earlier.

Moorhead has grouped the challenges facing organizations that consider joint ventures or mergers into six risk dimensions. These are (a) the structural complexity of merged companies, (b) the dynamic complexity of the industry, (c) complexity of the partners as it relates to corporate cultures, (d) compatibility of the partners in terms of trust, (e) alignment of goals and principles between the partners, and (f) the ability to handle alliance conflict. The ability of the partners to manage these risks has a significant impact on their chance of success (Moorhead, 1998). The cost of failure to manage these risks includes direct cost, cost of unwinding the venture, opportunity cost, bad marketplace reputation, and the Wall Street.

Moorhead speaks of partners - mergers rarely entail "partners" though some friendly mergers may be of that sort. Usually the management of one group dominates the other. The dominant takeover partner may keep some managers of the target firm, but they need not. It is of course true that the new management team faces the problem of integrating the cultures and processes of two different firms that, to some extent, are being combined. However, this effort might be minor for a conglomerate merger where the two merged parties operate along different business lines.

When Concert was dissolved, its customers and network infrastructures were divided between AT&T and BT (the two parent organizations). Some of the network infrastructures were shared for about three years. Concert's employees were divided into four groups. One group was absorbed into AT&T; a second group went to BT; a third group transferred into the Computer Sciences Corporation, (as an outsourcing company), and the fourth group consisting of about one third of the 6,000 employees were given a generous severance package.

To caution companies contemplating the formation of joint ventures, this study also presents some background information on previous attempts and failures of Concert's parent companies to form global alliances with other companies. This is to show some motivation for forming the joint venture. In Chapter 1, I present the history of Concert and information on AT&T and BT. In Chapter 2, 3, and 4 I present some applicable theories for analyzing organizational structure and operations. Specifically, Chapter 2 covers the rationale for the case study research paradigm and organizational theories; Chapter 3 describes the socio-technical systems theory and organizational development; while Chapter 4 offers theories of organizational change, management, leadership and triangulation protocols. Chapter 5 describes the applications of these theories to support the analysis of Concert development process and its compliance with the socio-technical system paradigm. A critical evaluation of the problems of the global joint venture and possible solutions is presented in Chapter 6.

In conclusion, Chapter 7 draws attention to ongoing merger activities during the last quarter of 2004 and advises the leaders of newly merged companies to learn from the Concert experience and exercise caution. I am confident that this critical analysis of the factors that led to the collapse of Concert can be beneficial to leaders of other large corporations who wish to establish joint ventures or alliances. Throughout this book, the terms "this researcher" and "this author" are used synonymously.

CHAPTER 1: HISTORY OF CONCERT

Background

Concert was a $10 billion global joint venture (GJV) of AT&T and British BT. Each of AT&T and BT owned 50% of Concert. Figure 1-1 illustrates Concert's global managed platform (GMP), a global network consisting of global points of presence (PoP) or clusters of switches located in different countries where Concert provided communication services. These PoPs, some of which are still in operation, are connected by international private line circuits (IPLCs), which are leased from various carriers around the world. The PoPs route communication traffic through the IPLCs.

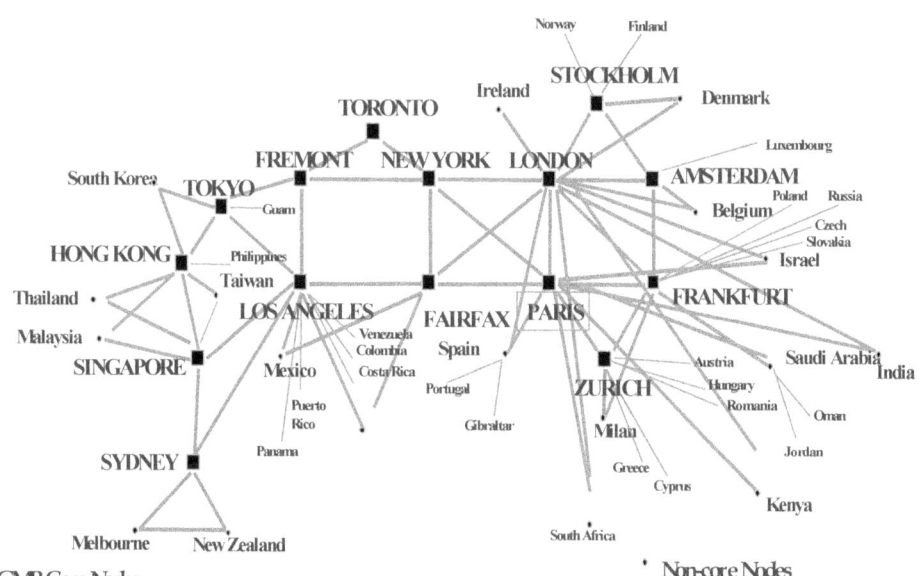

Figure 1-1
A global telecommunication network of Concert. (Source: Odubiyi, et. al., 2001)

The telecommunication service platforms include frame relay switches that support Concert's frame relay service, asynchronous transfer mode (ATM) switches supporting Concert's ATM services, and voice switches that support Concert's voice network services. ATM switches support the use of a single fiber cable to transfer three types of message traffic (i.e., voice, data, and images). This approach is more efficient than frame relay switches, which require a separate connection for each type of message traffic.

The GMP had over 1000 circuits (i.e., trunks) in over 52 countries. The network links that make up the GMP can be undersea cables, terrestrial (i.e., land lines), or satellites links. Concert had a direct sales force that served 29,000 multi-national corporations (MNCs) through its network of 47 distributors worldwide. Its frame relay network service served every major city in the US and the UK, and linked to an additional 170 cities in 61 countries.

Figure 1-2 describes the Telecom Operations' Map (TOM), the business process framework recommended by the TeleManagement Forum (TMF), an organization that represents telecommunications service providers. TMF is international not-for-profit organizations with the goal of helping telecommunication service providers automate their business processes to improve operational efficiency. Their objectives are to:

1. Provide guides on managing communication network functions.
2. Agree on the type of information and how information flows between functions.
3. Provide an environment that aids development of systems and products needed to automate business processes in the communications industry.

The organization has representatives from network service providers, operators, software, and equipment suppliers. The telecommunications industry has approved this framework for the Telecommunication Management Network (TMN) model. The model provides a logical way for viewing network service management and delivery. The TOM (in Figure 1-2) was developed from the basic TMN model. The model consists of network element management, network management, service management, and business management. The element management layer involves the management of network components such as switches, bridges, satellites, and relay stations. The network management layer covers the management of the processes required for the connected network elements and flow processes such as network planning, provisioning, and maintenance. The service management layer involves network service development and operations processes such as service planning and configuration. The business management layer supports processes that address customer care including order handling, customer problem handling, and billing. A selected group of individuals supports business management functions of the organization through interfaces with the customers.

    The TOM model provides a high level view of operations management. It can be applied to any communication service—wired or wireless. The use of a business process framework makes it easier for the Telecom Service Providers (TSPs) to analyze, evaluate, and improve the processes that can help them meet customer demands and profitability goals. While AT&T and BT employed the TOM model, initially Concert did not use this model in their management strategy.

Blueprint for a Crooked House

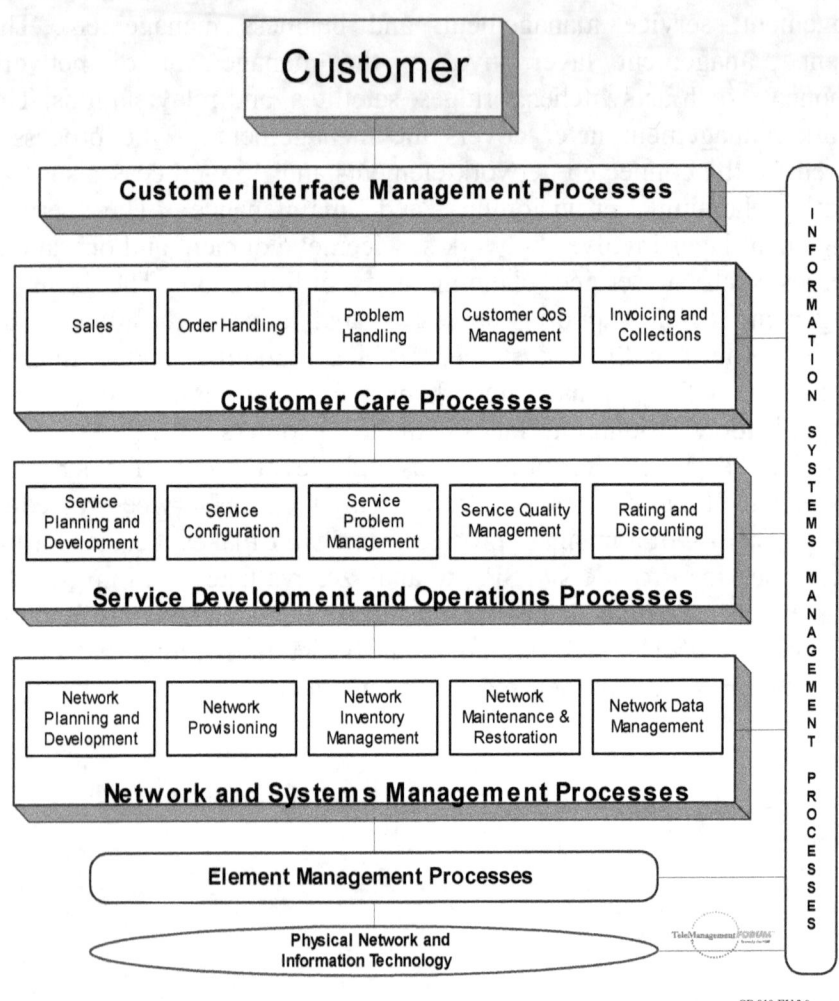

Figure 1-2
Telecom Operations Map (TOM): business process framework. (Source: By permission of The TeleManagement Forum, Bartorsky & Deland, 1999).

Prior Merger Experiences of this Author, BT, and AT&T

Prior to joining BT North America as a Research and Development Manager in 1996, this author spent about nine years in the aerospace industry with a single employer that went through two mergers. First, Loral Aerospace acquired its parent, Ford Aerospace in the early 1990s. This was followed by the acquisition by Lockheed Martin Aerospace of Loral Aerospace in 1995. The mergers were successful because there was synergy between the operations of the companies. In each situation, the acquiring company had a void that was filled by the acquired company. The success of the mergers was attributed to the fact that there were very few overlapping operations, which made it less [problematic] difficult to integrate necessary operations.

Background on BT and AT&T

BT, a UK company is one of the world's leading providers of telecommunication services. It provides local, long distance and international telecommunication services and Internet services. It serves more than 28 million exchange lines and provides network services to other licensed operators in the UK. BT used to be a monopoly in the UK but the US Telecommunications Act of 1996 forced telecommunication service providers to open their markets to competition and allowed the local companies to compete in all markets. To survive, BT developed a strategy to gain a foothold in the US market, where 50 percent of the dollar revenues in the telecommunication business was being generated. BT announced a merger with MCI in late 1996 and named the venture Concert[2] (Classic) an outgrowth of a $1 billion operation formed in 1993

---

[2] To separate the old Concert formed by BT and MCI in 1993 from the new Concert formed as a joint venture between AT&T and BT, the old Concert is referred to as Concert Classic. BT owned 75% of Concert Classic. BT's attempt to merge Concert

of which BT owned 75 percent and MCI owned 25 percent. The proposed merger failed because MCI was losing revenues and BT decided to reduce the amount offered MCI shareholders by $4 billion (from $21 billion to $17 billion). WorldCom, a US based company, then stepped in, outbid BT, and acquired MCI communications. BT profited from WorldCom's acquisition of MCI by receiving $7 billion for its stake in MCI. BT then started looking for another joint venture partner. Eventually, it narrowed the search to AT&T, Bell Atlantic (now Verizon Communications), Qwest, and Sprint.

In July 1998, BT selected AT&T as a 50-50 partner for a global joint venture called Concert. The old Concert was called Concert Classic while the new organization was called Concert. In this study, all references to Concert refer to the new Concert; a global joint venture of AT&T and BT. The name was selected to suggest global harmony for a premier global company. Hopes for success were high since AT&T had just got out of a failed partnership (i.e., World Partners) with several European telecommunication companies. Additional information on the profiles and business performance statistics on AT&T, BT and MCI are accessible respectively at http://att.com/att, http://www.btplc.com, and http://global.mci.com/about/mci.

Some Lessons Learned from the Failure of MCI-BT Merger

After the failure of the proposed MCI-BT merger attempt, Dan Moorhead (1998) developed a learning history document and presented the results to several senior managers at BT. In the document, he asserted that merger success requires success in both the development of merger strategy and implementation or operation of the resulting entity.

According to Moorhead, based on his analysis of the failed merger of Concert Classic and MCI, some of the positive lessons learned were that the perceptions in the marketplace of BT's global vision was

---

Classic with MCI between 1996 and 1998 but failed. BT then teamed with AT&T to form the new Concert.

positive. There was respect for the opinions of the leaders and BT had a strong strategy and plans. The parties involved believed that BT was serious about the merger and was not going through with the venture merely to improve its self-image. Some of the negative lessons learned were:

1. BT did not learn well from experience and did not disseminate what it knew effectively. Moorhead (1998) recommended that BT should hold workshops for its employees, conduct action learning by performing after action reviews, and hold concurrent and retrospective learning histories.

2. BT paid a heavy price for not having a contingency plan for any possible failure of the venture. BT was also advised to use scenarios analysis to prepare for different forms of failures and develop and use the best alternative to a negotiated agreement.

3. BT submerged conflicts to fudge merger issues. BT was advised to confront differences quickly, without giving in, and to use third party advisors when required.

4. BT emphasized development of relationship at the expense of addressing concrete implementation issues. It was therefore advised to use principled negotiation strategies, confront unprincipled tactics, be trustworthy (but not fully trusting), and to separate relationship issues.

5. BT also needed to address the "soft" variables, such as relationship building and repair, nurturing of trust, and openness to cross cultural learning. While it is difficult to quantify these soft variables, they are critical to the success of any joint venture.

Moorhead also recommended that in any future merger and joint venture activities, BT needed to refine its strategy, align the new organization to the strategy, build an organization culture to support it, and get people to deliver the results. He reported that the 75 percent failure rate in global mergers and acquisitions is caused primarily by failures in implementation of the merger and not in the strategy. To manage risk, he recommended that BT should develop working relationship with the new partner to ensure that BT is counted among the 25 percent successful global mergers.

In the view of this author, BT has what Jim Collins (2001) called a "Culture of Discipline". Such a culture is very effective in moving a company from "Good to Great" as defined by Jim Collins (2001). While BT had the motivation to implement all the recommendations listed above, it was rather difficult to transfer such a culture to an offspring in a joint venture when a third party was involved.

Concert Business Story and its Activation as a Global Joint Venture

Concert officially opened its doors in January 2000 after 18 months of organizational design by AT&T and BT personnel. Prior to January 2000, Concert was a wholly-owned subsidiary of BT. Concert provided complete global communications to about 270 multinational corporations (MNCs) and the international calling needs of individuals and businesses around the world. The goals of the joint venture included (a) offering communications services on a large scale with a high level of quality; (b) combining the trans-border assets and operations of each company, (including their existing international networks), all of their international traffic, international products for business customers; (c) generating revenues of over $7 billion during the year 2000 and EBITDA (i.e., earning before interest, tax, depreciation, and amortization) of over $1 billion; and (d) employing a staff of about 6,000. (Concert, 1999). The joint venture had the enormous task of integrating complex social and technical systems of the parent companies.

Motivations, Purpose and Significance of this Study

What factors contributed to the failure of the $10 billion global joint venture (Concert Global Networks) between AT&T and BT, and what lessons could be learned from this experience?

While there are several benefits of strategic (i.e., cooperative) alliances between small and large corporations at the national and global scales, Hutt, Stafford, Walker, and Reingen (2000) attribute the failure of many alliances to *inattention* to personal relationships between the employees of the partnerships. Some of the benefits identified include opening new markets, gaining new competencies, sharing risks, exploiting synergies, and conserving resources. Partners tend to emphasize the technical aspects of the alliance while ignoring the importance of people's values (p. 51).

Three approaches identified as necessary to effect collaboration among the partners are (a) establishing communication among the team members at the corresponding levels of managerial responsibility, (b) identifying the types of communications that unite partners and ameliorate conflicting beliefs, and (c) establishing trust among participants from both teams. Michael Skapinker (2000) in a *Financial Times* analysis expresses his concern at the pace of mergers and acquisitions contrary to the evidence that many of them fail, leaving the shareholders with poor returns on their investments. In Skapinker's view, "Mergers of equals can be so dangerous because it is not clear who is in charge" (FT, April 12, 2000). In the same article, Colin Price, a partner at McKinsey, the management consultants who specialize in mergers and acquisitions, attributes the reasons for the failures to poor implementation. He also claims that in about half of failed mergers, the fault is due to senior management's failures to consider different cultures of the companies involved. Peter Martin (2001) in another FT report attributes the failures of several European companies attempts to merge with American companies to a clash of cultures. Skapinker cites the survey results of Mark Sirower, a visiting professor at New York University, an advisor to the Boston Consulting Group, and the author of *The Synergy Trap* (Skapinker, 2000) that 65 percent of mergers fail to benefit shareholders. For global mergers, the failure rate is placed at 75 percent, and 90 percent for Fortune 50 companies (Moorhead, 1998a). This is due in part to the fact that mergers expose the strategy of the companies that are merging to the competitors, thereby helping the competitors to develop their own strategies to remove any negative impacts of the mergers on their organizations.

This observation is reinforced by a published statement in the February 8 edition of *Los Angeles Times* in which Jack Welch, the former General Electric (GE) Chairman told Hewlett-Packard (HP) Chairwoman Carly Fiorina that he sees some deficiencies in HP's plan to acquire Compaq Computer Corporation for $22.5 billion. Competitors can readily exploit these deficiencies. Jack Welch sees the deficiencies as the reason why European regulators approved the deal while rejecting GE's bid to buy Honeywell. Welch said, "Your competitors want this deal to go through. It will create chaos. They will clean both your clocks while you are doing all this" (Reuters, 2002). HP acquired Compaq for $19 billion in 2002 with the hope of being the leader in the PC business but it is still struggling to catch up with Dell Inc., a company that has not made any significant acquisition (Emily Thornton, *Business Week*, 12/06/2004). "Two years after the merger, HP still needs to prove it can execute its broad strategy otherwise pressure will build for its breakup" (Ben Elgin, *Business Week*, 12/13/2004; p. 98).

According to Thomson Financial Securities Data (Skapinker, 2000) during the first quarter of 2000, companies around the world spent about $1,166 billion on mergers and acquisitions. At 65 percent failure rate, a loss of $757.9 billion was expected from these activities. The companies involved in mergers and acquisition at the time were AOL and Time Warner, AirTouch's takeover of Mannersmann of Germany, the merger of SmithKline Beecham, and Glaxo Wellcome, AT&T and BT's creation of Concert global joint venture. Also WorldCom's merger with MCI was just in its infancy. When WorldCom initiated their all-stock merger with MCI, their stock was trading at about $36 per share. At the time of this writing WorldCom had changed its name to MCI, which is just coming out of bankruptcy. At the time of the merger, BT's share was trading at about $200 per share. At the time when Concert was going through the dissolution process, BT's share was trading at about

$40. While one may not attribute all the losses to the mergers and acquisitions, the fact remains that AT&T and BT lost $10 billion in their joint venture. As explained by John Rendleman (2001) the loss is in equity that resulted in their participation in Concert. According to Sandra Palumbo as reported by Rendleman (2001), Concert lost a significant amount of revenue because the company was not able to capture new customers because of the confusion in complex relationship between AT&T and BT. It was not clear to the customers as to which carrier was responsible for specific services. As a result, the combined assets under performed due to unused telecommunication resource capacity.

Purpose of the Study

This case study employs critical reflection based on leadership theories, organizational change models, and cultural influences to analyze the factors that contributed to the failure of Concert—a $10 billion global joint venture of AT&T and BT.

Significance of the Study

Losses from mergers and acquisition have significant impacts on global economy and peoples' welfare due to loss of employment and poor returns on stakeholders' equity. This study provides some insights on why Concert is a good case study from which other companies contemplating mergers or joint ventures can learn. Over $100 billion worth of mergers and acquisitions were made during the last quarter of 2004 (Network World, 12/20/2004). The leaders of these companies can benefit from the lessons learned from the impact of leadership styles, organizational change management, and cultural influences from the Concert experience thereby avoiding the missteps reported in this study. If well established global conglomerates like AT&T and BT, with access to the best talents in the industry, can build a crooked house, then other companies are not immune.

Summary

Chapter 1 offers a brief history of Concert starting with its formation as a global joint venture through to its dissolution. The chapter also provides background information on AT&T and BT, and concludes with a presentation on the motivations, purpose, and significance of this study.

CHAPTER 2: STUDY ASSUMPTIONS, RATIONALE FOR SELECTING THE CASE STUDY APPROACH, AND ORGANIZATIONAL THEORIES

> *"If we all worked on the assumption that what is accepted as true is really true, there would be little hope of advance."*
> *Orville Wright*

Assumptions and Limitations of the Study

This study employs the case study approach, a qualitative research paradigm. It is therefore guided by the assumptions listed in column one of Table 2-1. In addition to understanding underlying assumptions, the researcher needs to identify some reasons for selecting a paradigm. Creswell (1994) proposed five criteria: (a) the researcher's philosophical worldview based on the assumptions listed in Table 2-1, (b) the researcher's level of knowledge and experience, (c) the researcher's psychological maturity (i.e., competence in conducting research), (d) the nature of the problem, and (e) audience for the study. Table 2-2 describes specific reasons for selecting a qualitative research paradigm. Selection of a qualitative paradigm--the case study approach is driven by the nature of the problem. Reflective analysis of the factors based on leadership and organizational change management theories are suitable for explaining the outcome of the phenomenon (i.e., the failure of the joint venture).

Table 2-1. Quantitative and Qualitative Assumptions

Assumption	Philosophical Question	Quantitative Paradigm	Qualitative Paradigm
Ontological assumption	What is the nature of reality?	The researcher can view reality objectively. Reality is simple and probabilistic.	Reality is subjective, complex, and diverse.
Epistemological assumption	What is the relationship of the researcher to that researched?	Researcher does not interact with what is being researched.	Researcher interacts with the subject of the research.
Axiological assumption	What is the role of value?	Unbiased and value free.	Biased with researcher's value heavily interjected.
Rhetorical assumption	What is the language of research?	Formal and based on set definitions to promote objectivity.	Informal, qualitative, and evolving.
Methodological assumption	What is the process of research?	Deductive, cause and effect. Design is static demanding that categories be isolated before study; context free; focused on generalizations to support prediction and explanation; accurate and reliable results are obtained by applying reliability and validity standards.	Inductive process, context rich; emerging design process in which categories are identified during research process; emerging patterns and theories are developed to promote understanding; accuracy and reliability are achieved through verification and confirmability.

Source: Based on Creswell (1994), p. 5, by permission of Sage Publications

Table 2-2. Rationale for Selecting a Research Paradigm

Criteria	Qualitative Paradigm
Researcher's training and experience	Literary writing, computing text analysis, and library skills
Researcher's psychological maturity	The researcher is comfortable with absence of specific rules and guidelines for conducting research, he is comfortable with ambiguous situations and he has plenty of time for the research
Nature of the problem	Research is exploratory with unknown variables, and without a theory base
Audience for the study	Naturalists—individuals supportive of qualitative research paradigm.

Source: Based on Creswell (1994), p. 9, by permission: Sage Publications

Case Study Research

A case study is the investigation of the characteristics and complexity of a system in order to understand the value of the case (Stake, 1995). Creswell (1998) defined a case study as "an exploration of a bounded system or a case" (p. 61). The exploration consists of detailed data collection from multiple sources over time. The system is considered bounded by time and place. In some cases, a case study may include multi-site data collection. Also, the context of a case study may not be limited to a physical location; it may include "social, historical and/or economic settings" (Creswell, 1998, p. 61). Stake (1995) proposed three foci for a case study: (a) intrinsic case study in which the goal is to understand a specific case, (b) an instrumental case study whereby the case is used as a tool to explain an issue or issues, and (c) collective case study used in a situation where the research involves multiple case studies.

Isaac and Michael (1989) defined the purpose of case study research as the in-depth study of the background, present status, and environmental influence of a specific social unit, an individual, a group, or an institution. They cited Piaget's studies of cognitive growth in children and "an intensive study of the inner-city culture and living conditions in a large metropolitan environment" (Isaac & Michael, 1989, p. 48) as examples.

Creswell (1998) considered the case study method as the most widely used approach in qualitative research because it is the most familiar. It is used for problem case analysis in medicine, for studying a case in law, and as case reports in political science. It is viewed as a multidisciplinary approach that has been traced back to the French sociologist LePlay's study of families and to research performed at the University of Chicago's Department of Sociology in the 1920s and 1980s (Creswell, 1998). Some notable contributors to the case study research include sociologists Thomas and Znaniecki in 1958 and educators Merriam, 1988; Yin, 1989; Hamel, 1993; and Stake, 1995 (cited in Creswell, 1998). Among the strengths of case study research are its utility for obtaining background information for planning major studies; its ability to identify important variables, processes, and interactions; and the possibility of using it as an example to describe more generalized statistical inferences. However, because of their narrow focus, Isaac and Michael (1989) cautioned that it might not be easy to generalize their results.

In selecting a type of case study research, the researcher is advised to decide whether the case is going to be based on a single or multiple cases (i.e., collective), within a site or multiple sites, devoted to a case or a single issue (i.e., intrinsic or instrumental). One could perform a case study to show different views on a problem, process, or event.

Data Collection and Analysis in Case Study Research

Case study research relies on extensive data collection from a variety of sources: interviews, documents, audio-visual materials, and so forth. Creswell (1998) recommends Yin's six characterizations of case study data: documentation, archival records, interviews, direct observations, and physical artifacts. While Yin considers holistic and embedded data analysis acceptable, Stake (1995) promotes a holistic approach. In holistic data analysis, all data on the case are analyzed, while only a part of the data is analyzed in the embedded approach. In Stake's view, detailed case description, thematic analysis, and case interpretation should emerge from the data collection process. A typical format for analyzing multi-case study is to perform a "within-case analysis followed by a thematic analysis across the cases—termed cross-case analysis" (Creswell, 1998, p. 63). The final step in case analysis is the development of a lessons-learned report.

Research Challenges in Case Study Research

Some of the critical issues that challenge case study researchers include the following (Creswell, 1998): The researcher must identify a well-bounded case while several other cases are likely candidates worth selecting. The researcher is expected to decide whether to select a single case, with the understanding that multiple cases will diminish the researcher's depth of analysis. While multiple cases aid the researcher in generalizing the final results, most qualitative researchers have little regard for generalizability. Since it may be difficult to define the start and end points for certain cases, it may be difficult to establish time, event, and process boundaries for a case.

These three research challenges do not pose any problems in this case study. The phenomenon is well bounded. The research focuses on a specific event, the creation and fall of the global joint venture. A single case is investigated. It is feasible to define the start and end points of the event.

This study describes Concert and the goals of the GJV. It presents Concert as a complex organization with non-routine tasks and unpredictable environment. As Stebbins and Shani (1998) have noted, non-routine organizations depend on "more non-linear transformation processes in core work areas, and have more departments that can be classified as non-routine" (p. 2). Non-routine organizational units perform non-routine tasks in unpredictable environments (Stebbins & Shani, 1998). This study also analyzes the processes employed in integrating workforces from British and North American cultures, and the technical systems of both organizations.

Assumptions on the Cultural Aspects of this Study

The cultural aspects of this study are limited to the influences of the European and American styles of management, human communication, and work styles. This situation may be different from other cultures such as the Japanese and American or the Chinese and Americans. The researcher has studied under both the British and American educational systems. The analysis of some of the factors is based on my conjectures and theories of leadership and organizational change management. As much as I tried to exclude any bias in the reflective analysis of the factors, in some of the observations it may not be possible to fully eliminate all the biases based on my background and experience.

Viewing Organizations as Complex and Open Systems

All operations within organizations fall into one of the four cells shown in Table 2-3. For routine tasks in a predictable environment, assumptions made during task planning will hold during enactment of the task. The workers do not need to learn any new skills. This is the situation with cell one.

Four assumptions embodying the classical view of organizational control typical of cell 1 are: A stable environment requiring changing a few parameters in the manager's decision model. Routine tasks at the managerial and operations level; the supervisors are knowledgeable and bureaucratic measures are dominant. The objective of the management control system is to control each worker and coordinate his or her activities.

The superiors and subordinates are assets with complete knowledge. They are viewed as work horses or money machines. (Birnberg, 1998, p. 28)

Table 2-3. Dimensions of Organizational Operational Context

Nature of Environment (Economic, Political, Cultural Forces)	**Nature of Task (Level of Complexity)**	
	Routine (Simple)	Non-routine (Complex)
Stable/Predictable	Cell one – Routine task in a stable environment	Cell Two – Non-routine task in a stable environment
Unpredictable	Cell three – Routine task in an unpredictable environment	Cell four – Non-routine task in an unpredictable environment

Source: Adapted from Birnberg (1998).

In cell 2, the individual is the object of control, a cog in the wheel of the organizational process. A stable environment and a non-routine task demand that the manager provide resources to aid learning so the worker can adapt and master the task. The knowledge should be made public to benefit all workers. (Birnberg, 1998, p. 28)

In cell three, where the task is routine but the environment is unpredictable, the manager needs to be open to changes and diverge from previous practices (Birnberg, 1998). Managers should be sensitive to changes in the environment.

The fourth cell provides the greatest challenge to most organizational researchers. "Most researchers in organizational control couch problems in cell 4 under the umbrella of uncertainty" (Birnberg, 1998, p. 40). The task and the environment are poorly defined in cell 4, and the manager needs to understand new system behavior to deal effectively with the situation. The success of the organization depends on the manager's ability to link strategic goals to operational goals such as profitability. Cell 4 models a situation in which the world is changing and tasks are non-routine, leading to a disorderly or complex system. Turbulence in the environment leads to stress in the system, and the manager must organize the company and its support systems to simultaneously achieve two goals: learn and adapt (Birnberg, 1998, p. 31). "Learning is easiest when one is free to experiment with alternative behaviors in a controlled environment without dealing with environmental instability or noise" (p. 31). The environment is easier to understand when the problem is easy. In cell 4 when the environment is uncertain and the task is difficult, the nature of organizational planning and control is complex. Therefore, an integrated view of organizational control system is required.

Like most organizations, Concert's business processes were complex and they operated in open and uncertain cultural, economic, and political environments. As described in Table 3, Concert operated primarily in the fourth cell as a non-routine organization. Most of the functions performed by a significant number of the departments (e.g., network planning, provisioning, management, and delivery) were non-routine. These activities were performed in a competitive global marketplace characterized by unpredictable economic, cultural, and political environments.

The Issue of Organizational Control

The next task is to develop strategies for "controlling" the task, the individual, and the organization. The term <u>controlling</u> (Birnberg, 1998) is placed in quotation marks because, given all the uncertainties involved; one cannot claim to control all the variables that affect organizational behavior. All one can do is attempt to understand such behavior and use that knowledge to guide organizational decision-making (Hallinan, 1997). To effectively control organizational processes, one needs to understand the nature of the task and the environment.

Table 2-4. Understanding Organizational Control Issues

Characteristic	Cell 1	Cell 2	Cell 3	Cell 4
Degree of uncertainty	Lowest	Moderate (task)	Moderate (environment)	Highest
Control system	Mechanistic	Converging	Flexible	Fluid
Focus of control system	Autonomous (Individual)	Individual and task	Individual, task, and environment	Group task and environment
Issue for control	Procedures/ outcomes	Outcome, learning/ feedback	Outcome, recognition, adaptation	Learning, group adaptation
Role of trust/ cooperation	Minimal	Low	Medium	High
Degree of formality	High	Fairly high	Fairly high	Low

Note: This table includes materials adapted from Birnberg, (1998).

Organizational Control Issues for Complex Organizations

Table 2-4 explains control challenges faced by organizational managers who must operate at varying levels of uncertainty. "Non-routine organizational units face a high number of exceptions or uncertainties (unexpected situations with frequent problems) in the course of carrying out work where problem resolution is complex or unknown at the outset" (Stebbins & Shani, 1998, p. 2). Column 5 in Table 2-4 identifies organizational control requirements for complex organizations like Concert.

Typical of non-routine organizations, Concert was composed of a social subsystem (the employees with knowledge, skills, attitudes and other human elements), a technical subsystem (the inputs and the technology that convert inputs to outputs), and the environment subsystem (which included customers, competitors, and the global economic and political landscape). The design of Concert as an organization aimed to integrate the three subsystems with an effective strategy, nonlinear transformation processes, efficient organizational structure, and organizational support processes to ensure the company's survival. In essence, it needed to comply with the assumptions underlying socio-technical systems theory.

Summary

Chapter 2 covers the case-study approach—a qualitative research paradigm for analyzing the operations of an organization plus the research challenges in using the approach. The chapter identifies organizational control issues and emphasizes the importance of managing organizations as complex and open systems that make them unstable.

CHAPTER 3: SOCIO-TECHNICAL SYSTEMS THEORY AND ORGANIZATIONS

Socio-technical Systems Theory

Socio-technical Systems theory (STS) assumes that organizations need to coordinate social, technological, and economic dimensions to survive (Scott, 1998). STS is a philosophy as well as a method. Philosophically, it supports the concept of empowerment and the links between product and customer. As a method, it provides a reasoned approach to organizational improvement (Taylor & Felten, 1993).

Background on Socio-technical Systems

The three most important branches of organization theory have been identified as the rational model, the human relations model, and the systems model (Flood & Carson, 1993, p. 79). The rational model of the organization is based on three theories: (a) administrative management theory, (b) scientific management theory, and (c) Max Weber's bureaucracy theory. This model views the organization as an instrument for achieving the goals and objectives of those who establish it.

The human relations model addresses three issues: the social nature of people at work, individual motivation, and leadership. It "puts people and their needs at the center of analysis of organizations" (Flood & Carson, 1993, p. 80).

The systems model views organizations as complex systems with interrelated parts. Because the parts are closely related, the system must be studied as a whole (i.e., a holistic view rather than a reductionistic view is proposed) to explain organizational behavior (Flood & Carson, 1993, p. 80). Organizations are considered to be open systems; therefore, to survive they must adapt to environmental changes by satisfying four functional or survivability imperatives: (a) adaptation to changing environment, (b) goal-attainment (i.e., purposeful existence or goal-drivenness), (c) integration of the organization's resources with those of its environment, and (d) latency or self-maintenance (Parsons & Smelser, cited in Flood & Carson, 1993, p. 80).

Development of Socio-technical Systems Theory

Socio-technical systems theory (STS) (Pasmore & Sherwood, cited by Flood & Carson, 1993, p. 80) and contingency systems theory (CST) (Lawrence & Lorsch, cited by Flood & Carson, 1993, p. 80) are variants of the systems model. While the systems model is based on theoretical insights, STS and CST theories are based on empirical research. STS theory proposes that an organization's main goal is best attained only if its social, technical, and economic aspects are optimized together and built around autonomous work groups.

STS theory was developed at the Tavistock Institute of Human Relations in England after the Second World War. Researchers at the Institute were influenced by human relations research in the United States. They conducted several studies in different work settings, looking for ways to improve productivity and worker morale. Their approach was termed "action" research because the researchers collaborated with management and labor to introduce changes into the work environment and to measure outcomes of the new modes of operation (Jaques, cited in Scott, 1998, p. 113). Researchers were able to identify unique features of organizations as both social and technical systems. "Their core interface consists of the relation between a non-human and a human system" (Trist, quoted in Scott, 1998, p. 113).

Rather than demand that human and social units conform to technical demands of the operations, the STS approach recognizes the need for both. Since the social and technical components of organizations follow different laws, instead of looking for the best of each, joint optimization of the system is emphasized (i.e., a coupling of dissimilar components). The Tavistock research team went against the conventional management mind-set of the time (the 1950s). While the prevailing management styles of that time recommended top-down, manager-controlled, technical bureaucracies, the Tavistock team pushed for systems that promoted "discretionary behavior, internalized regulation, and work group autonomy" (Trist, quoted in Scott, 1998, p. 114).

Organizations as Socio-technical Systems

All organizations are viewed as socio-technical systems because they are composed of a technical subsystem to produce a product or render a service, and a social subsystem for managing the activities of the participants to achieve the goals and survival of the organizations (Taylor & Felten, 1993). STS are based on four basic principles:

1. Some organizations exist with a purpose well understood by all participants. Such organizations are considered purposeful. Others are considered "purposive" because they claim to have missions but no one understands what they are (Taylor & Felten, 1993, p. 2).

2. Some organizations are product or output focused because they emphasize activities or processes.

3. Managers and labor leaders recognize the uncertainties in their environment and are convinced that the old mechanistic organizational models are no longer effective.

4. The best organizational design goals are bound to fail if commitment among all participants throughout the organization is not obtained.

The fourth principle explains why organizations emphasize compliance. The goal of compliance theory is to employ different compliance structures (i.e., coercive, remunerative, and/or normative) to gain commitment from members of organizations (Etzioni, 1975). The following paragraphs present the use of STS to balance the technical, social and environmental demands of organizational systems.

Organizational Systems: Balancing the Technical, Social, and Environmental for Survival

Organizational systems must balance technical, social, and environmental elements in order to survive. Figure 3-1 describes the socio-technical components of an organization.

Viewing an organization as a system requires an identification of the organization's mission (i.e., the values that it creates to justify its existence), its managers' philosophy, and the values that underlie their mission. One should also identify the relationships between the organization and the various interested parties with which it interacts. The environment in Figure 3-1 consists of economic, political, and cultural forces. A review of the organization as a system needs also to determine its inputs, outputs, and physical and technological boundaries. This will help identify organizational problems, needs, and areas to improve.

Figure 3-1.
An organization as a Socio-Technical System (STS).

An organization could also be viewed as the interaction of four highly interrelated variables: tasks or processes that convert inputs to outputs, people or human resources, organizational structure or the roles of the participants, and the technology used to convert inputs to outputs. The four interrelated variables can be modeled as two interdependent open systems—the social and the technical systems. To produce anything, the two systems must interact with the environment. In any organization, the technical system comprises materials, machines, and processes used to convert inputs to outputs (Fox, 1995, p. 92). The technical system must adjust to stresses and strains imposed by the environment. Its survival depends on how well the organization can self-regulate its properties.

The Technical Perspective of the Organization

The technical or technological aspect of an organization is defined on the basis of its inputs and outputs instead of tools, processes, or techniques. The technical system excludes the job descriptions, as well as supervisory and other control systems. Fox (1995) describes eight important features of the technological (i.e., technical) aspect of an organization:

1. The properties of the materials being produced such that a quality standard can be ensured.

2. The immediate work environment, such as lighting, noise, dust, and temperature, must be controlled.

3. The spatio-temporal distribution of the machines, workers, and processes (simultaneous or sequential performance of operations) must be defined.

4. The level of mechanization or automation must be defined.

5. The grouping of operations must be known.

6. Those processes that are necessary versus those that are optional must be recognized.

7. The type and location of repair operations must be publicized to reduce down time.

8. The logistics on material supply processes to support the

operations and to distribute the final product to the consumers must be known. (p. 93).

The Social Perspective of an Organization

The social view of an organization consists of the role expectations and work-related interactions of those in positions most involved with balancing the organization's activities. This includes cooperation and coordination among organizational participants. Fox (1995) also identifies the following six important requirements of the social aspect of STS:

1. Work roles should be organized to identify cooperation or competition among workers.

2. Work rules are organized to promote ownership of results.

3. The work teams should share the responsibility for delivering supporting materials to workers.

4. Workers should have easy access to resources with limited control of the resources by managers and workers.

5. Workers should be encouraged to collaborate to reduce failures in operations.

6. Workers should feel empowered with enriched roles (p. 93).

Managers need to maintain a balance between coordination and control of workers. Technical systems control follows the laws of natural sciences, while the control of social systems follows the laws of human sciences (Fox, 1995).

Designing Socio-technical Systems

Socio-technical systems have been employed in several industrialized countries to improve productivity and human well being in organizations. Unfortunately, in most applications work systems were assumed to be linear and well defined. Well-defined linear systems consist of routine tasks with sequential processes for converting inputs to outputs. However, most organizational systems are ill defined with multiple conversion processes (Fox, 1995). They are nonlinear systems. Fox then asserts that:

> The goal of designers of STS is to design an architecture of structure sustaining and reinforcing the development of interactive relationships which support and reinforce each other with respect to all functional requirements such as flexibility, delivery time, throughput time, product quality, innovative capacity, pollution control, quality of work and industrial relations. (Fox, 1995, p. 99).

In analyzing the elements of an organization (i.e., system, technical, and social) Fox (1995) advocates the use of *action research*, whereby organizational participants and other stakeholders are encouraged to express their views on organizational mission, management philosophy, values held by the organization, and work systems design. Fox also recommends that a socio-technical systems design process should follow an iterative and continuous action-research-based process, which is deemed as critical to implementing any socio-technical system.

Table 3-1. Comparison of the Socio-technical Model with the Traditional Model

Old	New
Technology first	Joint optimization of systems
People as extension of machines	People as complements to machines
People as expendable spare parts	People as a resource to be developed
Maximum task breakdown, simple, narrow skills	Optimal task grouping, multiple, broad skills
External controls: procedures, supervisors, specialist staffs	Internal controls: self-regulating subsystems
More organization levels, autocratic style: unilateral goal setting, assignment of workers	Fewer levels, participative style: Bilateral goal setting, selection of workers
Competitive gamesmanship	Collaboration, collegiality
Organization's purposes only (often with poor understanding/acceptance at lower levels)	Members' and society's purposes also (with good understanding/acceptance at lower levels): shared vision and philosophy
Frequent alienation: "It's only a job"	Commitment: "It's my job, group, and organization
Tendency toward low risk taking, mal-adaptation	Tendency toward innovation, adaptation
Less individual development opportunity and employment security	More individual development opportunity and employment security

NOTE: This table includes materials adapted from Taylor, Gustavson, & Caster, as cited in Fox (1995), p.102.

Table 3-1 presents a comparison between a socio-technical and traditional model of an organization.

Summary

Chapter 3 presents the theory and benefits of socio-technical systems and approaches for coordinating the social, technological, and economic dimensions for the survival of an organization.

CHAPTER 4: LEADERSHIP, ORGANIZATIONAL CHANGE MANAGEMENT THEORIES, AND TRIANGULATION PROTOCOLS

Organizational Leadership Issues and Change Management in Mergers and Acquisitions

To effectively address the problems of complex systems, management should rely on approaches that acknowledge interdependencies in strategic planning, management, and operational control processes. In a Viewpoint column in *Financial Times* "Why mergers are not for amateurs" Knowles-Cutler and Bradbury (2002) reports the results of a research conducted by Deloitte & Touche that aimed to determine whether the failures of companies are due to mergers and acquisition activities or the general economic conditions. In investigating 40 companies, the study found that 57 percent of the companies failed because of mergers or acquisitions and not because of the prevailing business climate. The blame was placed at the footsteps of the leaders. Their findings identify such factors as ill-conceived rationale behind the deal, which resulted in over payment for the deal, poor strategic fit for the business, serial acquisitions to hide failures in previous acquisitions, inattention to integration of the operations after the deal was signed, and the failure of management. The research results also credit strong leadership with the ability to make strong decisions early as the major factors required for the most successful mergers such as that of BP with Amoco. The report also identifies delays in selecting managers with clearly specified roles and responsibilities, and development of clear strategies for change management and cultural integration. The study finds that these *soft functions,* though critical to the success of the mergers and acquisitions, are usually ignored while emphasizing the value of facility closures and reduction of the workforce.

The findings of Deloitte & Touche reinforce the conclusions of Hutt, Stafford, Walker, and Reingen (2000) from a case study on the social network of a strategic alliance that partners tend to emphasize the technical aspects of the alliance while ignoring the importance of people's values (p. 51). Three approaches identified as necessary to effect collaboration among the partners are (a) establishing communication among the team members at the corresponding levels of managerial responsibility, (b) identifying the types of communications that unite partners and ameliorate conflicting beliefs, and (c) establishing trust among participants from both teams.

The following paragraphs will present organizational change management and leadership theories and underlying assumptions required for successful organizational leadership and change management and their impacts on merger and acquisition processes. The possible use of a socio-technical system approach to provide the answers will be investigated.

Managing Three Levels of Organizational Change with STS

Three approaches for enacting change in an organization are (a) deploying a new technology; (b) employing new people; and (c) starting new organizational structure, new policies, or new processes (O'Hara, Watson, & Kava, 1999). In addition to different types of change, each change can be implemented at different levels. O'Hara and his colleagues propose viewing organizations as socio-technical systems to help understand the complex interactions between technology and people (p. 64). They argue that every organization is a collection of interrelated parts, social and technical, where (a) people perform tasks; (b) tasks produce goods and services; (c) communication channels, authority, and workflow systems determine an organization's structure; and (d) technology serves as a problem-solving tool (e.g., computer systems). A distinction is made between a technical system and technology in an organization. The technical system consists of the technology and tasks performed to achieve organizational goals. While technology may be the same in different organizations, the technical system is the outcome of the application of technology. Each order of change in the three-order change is linked to a component of the STS model.

First-order change or alpha change deals with the changes initiated in task accomplishment, such as automating the process. An example is switching from manually sorting envelopes to an automated sorting process. First-order change is the lowest order of organizational change typically realized through technology application. Second-order change or beta change relates technology to tasks and people who perform them. For example, the introduction of word processors has changed the nature of work. The function of the secretary within the organization has changed. Instead of relying on secretaries to perform all typing activities, most employees do their own typing. Technology changes the method used to perform the tasks as well as the procedures. The approach used to interact with technology also changes.

Third-order change or gamma change deals with changes in people, tasks, communication authority, and workflow structure. Reengineering management structure and workflow is an example of a third-order change. Gamma order change is the highest order of organizational change resulting from technology introduction. Third-order change is known as the STS model when extended to cover the effect of "technologically induced change" (O'Hara, Watson, & Kava, 1999, p. 66). It is also known as the socio-technical change impact (SCI) model. Dimensions of successful change management by the project manager, project team, and the organization for each type of change are depicted in Table 4-1 on the following page.

Table 4-1. Dimensions of Successful Change Management

Dimension	Alpha Change	Beta Change	Gamma Change
Project Manager			
Management	Participatory	Facilitating	Empowerment
Business acumen	General understanding	Recognized specialized functional understanding	Recognized superior general and functional understanding
Technical ability	Specialist	Generalist	Futurist
Project Team			
Orientation	Technical specialist	Training specialist	Organizational design specialist
Level of communication	Project status; implementation planning guide	Project status; implementation planning guide; workflow walk-through; job behavior changes defined and reward structures altered	Project status; implementation planning guide; workflow walk-through; job behavior changes defined and reward structures altered; organizational preparedness; early successes publicized
Organization			
Attitude toward change	Understanding	Enthusiastic	Mobilizing
Implementation training	Task oriented	Task and role oriented	Task, role, and organizationally oriented
Problem handling	Supervisory	Middle management	Executive
Prob. Response	Immediate	Methodical	Introspective

NOTE: This table includes materials adapted from O'Hara, Watson, and Kava (1999), p. 70.

In Table 4-1, Concert operated at the beta change level at the project manager, project team, and organization level while because of the complexity of the organizational processes.

Table 4-2. Empowerment: Choosing Centralization or Decentralization

Factors affecting where decisions are made	Centralization is desirable when...	Decentralization is desirable when...
Decision Information	Using remote information is valuable in decision-making, and the information can be communicated to central decision makers at moderate cost.	Local decision makers have access to important information that cannot be easily communicated to central decision makers. Or Remote information is not valuable in local decision-making. Or Remote information is valuable in decision-making and is very inexpensive to communicate.
Trust	Central decision makers do not want to (or cannot) trust local decision makers for important decisions.	Local decision makers do not want to (or cannot) trust central decision makers for important decisions.
Motivation	Local decision makers work harder or better when told what to do by someone else (likely to be less common in the future).	Local decision makers work harder or better when they make decisions for themselves (likely to be more common in the future).

NOTE: This table includes materials adapted from Malone (1997), p. 30.

Empowerment

One major decision a manager needs to make is to determine the level of control to exercise over the workers—the issue of empowerment. Malone's (1997) suggestion on when to centralize decision making versus when to empower the workers (depicted in Table 4-2) can be helpful in implementing an STS. The table identifies the factors that affect where decisions are made. Three factors—decision information, trust, and motivation—"are important in determining the economic desirability of making decisions in different places" (Malone, 1997, p. 28).

Decision information is critical to making good decisions. Managers delegate when they trust subordinates; otherwise, decision-making is centralized. People are motivated when they have a say in decisions that affect what they do.

In Search of a Working Leadership Model for Organizational Change Management

Given the reinforcing assertions from several researchers that failures of mergers and acquisitions or joint ventures are caused by poor leadership (Moorhead, 1998; Hutt, Stafford, Walker, & Reingen, 2000; and Knowles-Cutler & Bradbury, 2002), therefore, it is important to present what leadership researchers and practitioners recommend about effective leadership. The following paragraphs present new developments in five areas on leadership: (a) leadership perspectives, (b) leadership development, (c) leadership and organizational change, (d) leadership practices, and (e) influences of the differences in management styles between Europe and North America. By reviewing the views of leadership researchers in these areas, this author can then analyze the Concert leadership model and evaluate its effectiveness and its possible contribution to the failure of the global joint venture.

The first group of authors who present different views of organizational leadership in four articles are Smith (1997) who holds the view that leadership is a living system, Kenney and Schwartz-Kenney (1996) identify implicit leadership theories believed to be determinants of leadership traits, Schein (1996) considers three cultures of management that are viewed as key to organizational learning, and Duke (1998) considers a normative context as necessary for effective organization leadership.

A second group of authors in four articles cover strategies for leadership development. Schriesheim (1997) emphasizes the importance of substitutes-for-leadership theory in leadership development, McNally and Gerras (1996) draw from their teaching experience at the US Military Academy at West Point to propose how approaches used for developing military leaders are also appropriate for developing civilian leaders. Fulmer, Gibbs, and Goldsmith (2000) present effective leadership development styles of winning companies while Gregersen, Morrison, and Black (1998) present what they consider as essentials for developing leaders for the global marketplace.

A third group of authors in five articles shed some lights on the challenges of change management in organizations. Dent and Goldberg (1999) propose strategies for challenging resistance to change in organizations. Harari (1999) attempts to explain why leaders avoid change, while Carroll and Hatakenaka (2001) explain with the aid of a case study, a strategy for driving organizational change in the midst of crisis. Beer and Eisentat (2000) provide some insights on what they consider to be silent killers of strategy in an organization followed by Beinhocker's (1999) scholarly treatise on robust adaptive strategies applicable to most organizational management settings.

A fourth group of authors in three articles present the practice of leadership. Fulmer and Wagner (1999) describe a set of leadership practices among selected organizations considered to have outstanding leaders and recommend approaches worth learning. Kirchmeyer (1998) describes what are viewed as determinants of managerial career success, while Rockart, Earl and Ross (1996) propose what they consider as eight imperatives for the new IT organization.

Dickson (2000) presents the views of several researchers and practitioners on the differences between the European and American management styles and their influences in organizational leadership. Peter Martin (2001) considers a clash of organizational management cultures as the most likely reason for endemic failures of mergers between the European and American companies.

Each of the five developments in organizational leadership is elaborated in the following paragraphs with the expectation that a cohesive approach to organizational leadership can emerge.

Leadership Perspectives

Citing Peter Senge's research Smith (1997) lists the following five disciplines as critical to learning organizations: (a) personal mastery, (b) keeping mental models to improve the learner's learning ability, (c) maintaining a shared vision, (d) team learning, and (e) systems thinking. In addition, leadership in learning organizations is expected to know how to handle five unique leadership situations claimed to limit today's leaders. The five distinct situations claimed to require a leader's special skills are the ability to: (a) overcome obstacles and intervene decisively, (b) know how to define duties and operate consistently, (c) improve consistently, (d) innovate uniquely—discover new opportunities, and (e) integrate completely by focusing on priorities in complex situations. Knowles-Cutler and Bradbury (2000) reinforce the importance of these leadership skills in their report of the research results on mergers and acquisitions conducted by Deloitte and Touche.

Discussing their idea of the use of implicit leadership theory and citing results from other studies (Foti & Lord, 1987, cited in Kenney and Schwartz-Kenney, 1996) claim that once an individual is categorized as a leader using specific traits and behaviors, even when the individual's traits and behaviors change the classifier still views the individual as a leader. This may explain why even after autocratic and brutal political leaders such as Slobodhan Milosevic, former leader of Serbia and Augusto Pinochet of Chile still have passionate followers even after their fall from positions of power.

Normative View of Organizational Leadership

Duke (1998) considers the normative view of organizational leadership as largely consisting of four components: (a) the view of the members about the conditions within the organization that makes leadership a necessity, (b) the pervasiveness of the conditions or beliefs about the presence or absence of the conditions, (c) beliefs about the intentions of the leaders, and (d) beliefs about how leaders should behave to realize their intentions. The paper's author is hopeful that understanding these four components would aid in understanding the roles of members in organizational leadership. Duke primarily focuses on the contextual aspects of leadership. As he sees it, one cannot describe a leader without specifying the context such as political leaders, academic, or corporate leaders.

To support his point, Duke describes the views of renowned organizational leadership researchers such as Herbert Simon who views an organization from three dimensions: (a) as a rational system in which a group of people with highly specialized structure focuses on achieving specific goals; (b) a natural system view which emphasizes the cultural dimensions of the organization with less emphasis on the formal structures; and (c) organizations with informal structures where members share a common interest to ensure organization's survival. Duke also presents the views of Scott and Davis (1992) who see organizations as consisting of two structure—behavioral and normative. A normative structure includes values, norms, and expected roles of members and participants. Norms are defined as generalized rules that govern the behaviors of the members of the organization to enable attainment of organizational goals. The author also highlights the views of interaction leadership theorists (i.e., interactionist theorists) who emphasize the importance of interaction between the leader and leadership situations, and interactions between leaders and followers. Transactional leadership is said to require exchange relationship of valued things where what is valued depends on the self-interest of the participants. Transformational leadership describes the situation where the leader and the followers aspire to achieve a goal that is larger than their immediate personal interest.

Internal Integration and External Adaptation

Citing Schein's work (cited Schein, 1985; p.15), Duke (1998) describes two challenges that face all organizations--internal integration and external adaptation. The survival of an organization is said to depend on its ability to adapt to its environment (i.e., meet the needs and expectation of its environment) while resisting the forces of individual's self-interest. Internal integration demands that members value and pursue common organizational goals. Leadership will fail if efforts to address the demands of external adaptation conflict with internal integration and vice versa. The need for leadership is small when individuals possess a clear sense of organizational direction and are committed to it. This is the key to selling a shared vision (Malone, 1997).

Three Cultures of Management

Schein (1996) describes three cultures of management that need to be understood and aligned to realize effective leadership in an organization. The three cultures are operators' culture, the culture of engineers (i.e., technocrats), and the culture of executives. The culture of operators assumes that the success of an organization depends on the peoples' knowledge, skills, and commitment because most operations are interdependent. Therefore, operators must be able to collaborate across teams, must value open communication, mutual trust, and commitments. Assumptions of the engineering culture are based on the belief that engineers should be able to master nature. Challenging problems motivate them and they believe in solutions that reduce or eliminate the need for people. In their view, the ideal world consists of machines and processes. They prefer simple cause-and-effect thinking in quantitative terms. They do not seem to view the organization as a socio-technical system, a necessary situation for the survival of the organization. The executive culture base their values on financial survival and returns on shareholders equity. Most executives rely on their judgments rather than trust subordinates. They believe that the organization needs to operate like a team while demanding that individuals will be held accountable for their actions. They believe that the organization has to be hierarchical because hierarchy is a measure of status. Executives focus more on task and control and less on building relationships—the soft variables. Schein assumes that an ideal world for executives is that in which the people, machines, and processes work smoothly without the need for people.

Executives view people as necessary evil and not as essential value, which in Schein's view explains why they can close plants, eliminate thousands of employees to correct their own mistakes. The author concludes that until the executives, engineers, and operators realize that they use different assumptions and languages, the organization cannot survive.

Given the varying perspectives on leadership, it is helpful to see if these views play any roles in leadership development process.

Leadership Development

Schriesheim (1997) considers the need to recognize the existence of activities or work situations that do not require leadership. He defines substitutes-for-leadership as certain situational determinants that act to reduce subordinates' dependence on the leader. The author considers large government contracts with bureaucratic rules and regulation that may reduce leadership's influence on subordinates as an example of substitutes-for-leadership. Technology, which can reduce the need for leadership, is cited as another example. This however assumes that the participants are mature enough to perform their responsibilities without looking for someone to guide them. It is helpful for a leader to recognize such situations so as to expend his/her resources in areas where they are needed. Unfortunately, this practice appears to be employed by organizational leaders immediately after announcing mergers and acquisitions, the wrong context for such a leadership style (Knowles-Cutler & Bradbury, 2002).

Leadership Development in the Military

McNally and Gerras (1996) report on their leadership development process in the military, which is based on the assumption that people are taught to be leaders regardless of their traits or behaviors. This approach may work in the military but it may not work well in the civilian world unless the leaders make some adjustments in their transition from the military to the civilian world. This author has had some first hand experience with such leaders in the civilian world. The MITRE Corporation employs a significant number of retired military officers from the Armed Forces. While these officers were top performers in the military, a few of them had some problems adjusting to the civilian life. Unlike in the military where subordinates accept orders and carry them out without question, many of their civilian subordinates do not always accept orders without question. Such an attitude is difficult to accept by retired military officers in civilian organizational environments. This is not to say that their military leadership training is not useful in civilian environment. The individual's traits and other factors may contribute to the leader's behaviors.

The authors taught the course titled Military Leadership for a combined 17 years. The course content includes (a) experience of followership, (b) analysis of past and present leaders, (c) exposure to role models, (d) exposure to theory-based systematic leadership framework for analyzing complex, but realistic leadership situations. The teaching methods employed by the authors appear fairly comprehensive. The cadets are exposed to techniques for developing critical thinking skills, developing cognitive skills such as identifying ambiguity, assumptions, and value conflicts, evaluation of evidence; application of logic, generating alternative inferences, and developing reasoned judgment.

Leadership Development Styles at Top Performing Companies

Fulmer, Gibbs, and Goldsmith (2000) describe leadership development styles at some of the top performing companies around the world by describing the leadership training strategy employed by each company. GE trains its leaders through its GE Institute at Crotonville, New York. At the Institute, GE leaders in training generate new initiatives (e.g., the six sigma quality improvement program) that drive the organization. Arthur Andersen employs its worldwide Partner

Development Program to build its leaders as business advisors. Shell Corporation uses its Leadership and Performance Program (LEAP) worldwide within its Shell companies. The World Bank employs its Executive Development Program (EDP) for managers to train its leaders. The program at the World Bank enjoys collaboration with Harvard Business School, Stanford University, INSEAD in France, and IESE—The Graduate School of Business of the University of Navarra in Spain. World Bank managers attend five weeks of classroom training coupled with hands-on project experience. Leaders can benefit from these leadership development approaches. While Concert has neither a formal leadership development model to be presented later in this report, neither it nor its parents manage any leadership development program operated or supported at a level supported by the companies listed above.

Leadership Characteristics

Gregersen, Morrison, and Black (1998) recommend four personal leadership characteristics—emotional connection, integrity, duality of purpose, and business savvy and four strategies (i.e., foreign travel, diversified work force, training, and overseas assignment) which they consider essential for developing global leaders. To develop emotional connection, the leader needs to have sincere interest and concern for others, be able to listen to people, and understand different points of view. Having integrity involves possessing ethical behavior and loyalty to the company and not willing to compromise on personal and company standards. Duality of purpose means having the ability to balance tensions, knowing when to act and when to collect additional information. The leader also needs to have the capacity to handle uncertainty. Possessing business and organizational savvy implies the ability to recognize worldwide market opportunities. This author can relate to the specific examples provided as strategies for developing global leaders from his experience as an employee of a global communication communications company. Foreign travel places the leader in the middle of the country, its culture, political system, economy, and market. It is important to establish teams in which people with diverse background and perspectives work together. This promotes the concept of localization, which makes the nationals feel like stakeholders in the success of the organization.

Leadership and Organizational Change Management

Since organizations are open systems that are exposed to the influences of their environments, the structure of leadership needs to be dynamic to accommodate the changes within the organization. Unfortunately for the leader, not everyone within the organization would embrace changing from what they know to unknowns. Dent and Goldberg (1999) propose strategies for challenging resistance to change. Rather than define change as it relates to individuals within an organization, the authors contend that organizations define change as systemic (i.e., administrative, technological, or structural changes). In essence they recommend that all aspects of an organization should be considered an integral part of the organization and understand that any change made to a part of the system affects the whole system.

> *"When the pace of change outside an organization becomes greater than the pace of change inside the organization, the end is near."*
> John R. Walter, Former President of AT&T

Leaders' Difficulties with Change

Harari (1999) defines the role of a leader as one of helping the followers stop fixing new problems with old solutions but that of identifying new solutions necessary to handle new problems. This observation is in line with Albert Einstein's belief as described in Covey (1991) which states that the problem we face cannot be solved with the current way of thinking (i.e., current problem cannot be solved with current paradigms). This issue is considered to be the most important task a leader will face.

Harari (1999) provides the following reasons as to why it is difficult for leaders to change:

1. The belief that business lives need to be stable and predictable because humans believe that stability and predictability are the natural ways of things. He then cautions that due to changing factors our traditional focus on control and certainty of events would not work today due to technological advances, removal of global barriers, customer demands, and unorthodox competitors. He asserts that "perpetual change is both a given and a necessity in today's business environment" (Harari, 1999, p. 37). This assertion makes good sense when one views the organization and leadership as a living system.

2. His claim as to why change is difficult for managers because it frustrates and disappoints them relates to the previous point about why people resist change because it moves them out of their comfort zones. He asserts that management involves creating plans, setting goals, and making commitments to employees, customers, and stakeholders. The manager's inability to meet commitments typically leads to a loss of trust, which is very important in interpersonal relationships. Therefore, change should not be instituted without considering other factors that might affect the outcome of the task at hand.

3. The author's third point relates to the second point above—change also makes our knowledge obsolete, making our goals in doubt, current plans irrelevant, and commitments in trouble, leading to personal discouragement and frustrations. Harari holds the reasonable view that as long as people believe that knowledge is power, and change invalidates the knowledge, which robs people of power, resulting in a sense of losing control over their affairs, people will always have the tendency to resist change. It is therefore the leader's duty to prevent the situation where people feel they are powerless. This can be avoided by sharing the decision making process with the participants and educating

them about the change and why it is necessary.

Change as a Demanding Process

Harari also views change as a demanding process which makes people do a lot of work that they did not expect they have to do leading to high levels of emotional stress, increasing conflict, and valuing old patterns of behavior (i.e., the good old days syndrome). This is a major challenge for leaders who are responsible for changing people's behaviors, which is not an easy task.

Carroll and Hatakenaka (2001) use a case study to demonstrate that resolving crisis involves instituting a rapid response team structure that treats employee's problem as a company problem using three steps: (a) stop the situation, (b) stabilize it—people problem such as salary, benefits, and promotions, is handled as personnel matter, while interpersonal matters that involve supervisory relationship or personality conflicts are managed by the management team; and (c) develop a plan of action to resolve problems. The following lessons learned seem to be applicable to management at any company. To the senior managers the authors recommend as follows:

1. Solve problems together with people to gain their trusts and commitment.
2. Communicate frequently to all stakeholders.
3. Develop inquiry skills and be willing to change your mind.
4. Encourage employee participation through multiple forums.
5. Be patient because the seeds of change may take years to materialize.

The idea of encouraging employee participation, while noble, will succeed or fail depending on how it is practiced within the company. If management does not provide the resources to ensure its success or they schedule meetings only after regular work hours without compensating the employees for their time, the initiative is bound to fail. The authors do not consider the value of these issues as part of senior managers' roles.

They also recommend that line managers need to (a) abandon the old style of management by control and be confident enough to ask for help, (b) improve social skills, (c) build trust through secure relationship, fruitful actions, think strategic, and expect more changes. The authors suggest that informal leaders need to be true to themselves, they should ask for what they want, be persistent-- which may not work in all situations, give honest feedback, forgive honest mistakes, and develop new skills from new jobs (p. 76). The authors conclude that the success at the company was achieved through learning which yield new sensitivity to others' emotions, perceptions, and relationship. Their final observation and suggestions can be summarized by the blocked quote below:

> It is natural to want to declare victory and move on, but management organization recovering from crisis must avoid treating change as a project that has been completed (Caroll & Hatakenaka, 2001, p. 77).

Six Barriers to Organizational Change

In their research, Beer and Eisentat (2000) identify what they consider as the six barriers to organization change in priority order as: (a) disengaging laissez-faire senior management style, (b) unclear strategy and conflicting priorities, (c) in-effective senior management team, (d) poor vertical communication, (e) poor coordination across functions, businesses or borders, and (f) inadequate down-the-line leadership skills and development. They conclude that the six barriers could be overcome with efficient application of path-goal theory. They suggest six capabilities deemed critical to sustainable competitive success which are (a) employ a leadership style of top-down direction and upward influence, (b) establish clear strategy and priorities, (c) have effective top team with general management focus, (d) have an open vertical communication, (e) employ effective coordination—teamwork that links customers, products, and functions, and (f) groom mid-level managers for leadership roles.

As can be surmised from the strategies for change management above, there is no single solution for change management but the general framework proposed by Beer and Eisentat above could apply to most situations. The next section provides some examples on the practice of leadership.

Leadership in Practice

Fulmer and Wagner (1999) claim that their research has identified 13 findings considered significant, eight of which are:

1. Alignment of leadership with organization's strategic objective is critical. To meet new business challenges, efforts must be aligned with business drivers.

2. Recognition of the value of human resource development and business experience—education and learning should be emphasized.

3. Leadership competencies should be identified and updated through internal and external training. Traits of successful leaders should be identified to drive development of leadership competencies. Once the competencies are established, they should be consistent across organizations regardless of geographic boundaries or business units.

Leadership and Organizational Management Theories

4. Companies are encouraged to grow their own leaders instead of recruiting from the outside. However, the authors skip discussing the pros and cons of such a policy. Certain behaviors or mindset entrenched among the leaders of the organization might make them inflexible and closed to new ideas. There is the tendency to continue to pursue the old ways of doing things that are based on past successes, which may not be appropriate to the uncertainties of the new business environment.

5. Organizations' leaders are advised to emphasize action learning. Action learning employs real time business issues to form the foundation for learning. The authors claim that action learning provides more than knowledge and information because it also provides skills to apply the leaders' knowledge in uncertain or unfamiliar situations. However, the authors ignore the fact that action learning, just like case-based research limits the learner to the techniques or methodology used in the case and may not expose him/her to all the fundamental theories and assumptions necessary to understand all aspects of the subject matter. BT employs action learning in developing lessons learned from failed operations (Moorhead, 1998).

6. Organizations should integrate assessment, development, feedback, coaching, and leadership succession planning.

7. The human resource department should obtain support from top management level for sustaining leadership development process.

8. Successful organizations always assess the impact of their leadership development process by using a metric to measure effectives. This point would be more helpful to the reader if the authors had provided or suggested effective metrics to measure leadership development process.

Eight imperatives for IT Departments' Success

Rockart, Earl, and Ross (1996) propose what they consider to be eight imperatives for the Information Technology department to succeed. The most important imperative is the recommendation to achieve two-way strategic alignment by aligning IT group with organization's business strategy. Claiming that 50 percent of capital investment in the US is spent on IT, the authors recommend that the Chief Information Officer (CIO) must be a formal or informal member of the top management team. The IT department should contribute to management thinking; identify business threats, and opportunities. This was the situation in this author's company. The head of the IT department was a vice president within the organizational leadership team and he was responsible for contributing to strategic thinking within the organization.

Triangulation Protocols for Validating the Results of this Study

The information presented on Concert was collected from credible and dependable sources, two of the requirements for validating qualitative research (Creswell 1994). An in-depth analysis of Concert has been presented based on data collected from multiple sources (i.e., data from company surveys and employees).

Triangulation protocols will be used in the following paragraphs to validate the results of this research. Triangulation protocols—the process of using more than one source to confirm research results (Stake, 1995)—are the most effective approach for validating qualitative research. Four triangulation protocols proposed by Norman Denzin in 1984 (cited in Stake, 1995) to increase confidence in the interpretation of results: data source triangulation, investigator triangulation, theory triangulation, and methodological triangulation will be used in this analyzing the results.

A Brief Review of Triangulation Protocols

In employing *data source triangulation* the researcher verifies that the data source remains unchanged at different times or as different participants interact differently. Data source triangulation helps to determine that what is being observed and documented holds the same meaning when circumstances change. The second protocol is *investigator triangulation*, which demands that other researchers observe the same phenomenon to determine if they report any differences in their observations. It is expected that incorporating the inputs of other researchers will help validate original data and in addition enlarge the amount of data for the study. The third protocol is *theory triangulation*, which promotes addition of multiple investigators or reviewers from different theoretical perspectives to participate in the research and compare observed data. For example, one researcher could be a behaviorist while the other could observe the phenomenon from a holistic perspective. Stake (1995) asserts that as long as the interpretations of the theorists are similar in meaning, they have achieved some degree of theoretical triangulation. *Methodological triangulation* is the fourth and the most widely used protocol (Stake, 1995, p. 114). This protocol asserts that multiple methods, such as reviewing old records after analysis of current observations, will increase confidence in the data used for the research. This research will employ data source, investigator, and methodological triangulation to validate any concluding assertions.

Summary

Chapter 4 provides a review of the literature on organizational leadership issues and change management from four leadership perspectives--leadership, development, change management, and the practice of leadership. The chapter closed with a description of triangulation protocols and its use for validating the findings from a qualitative study.

CHAPTER 5: ANALYSIS OF CONCERT'S ORGANIZATIONAL DEVELOPMENT PROCESS

Compliance with the Phases of STS Design and Leadership Models

The STS design process (Stebbins & Shani, 1998; Taylor & Felton, 1993) is depicted in Figure 5-1 below. The diagram is an expanded application of the STS framework described in Figure 3-1 in Chapter 3.

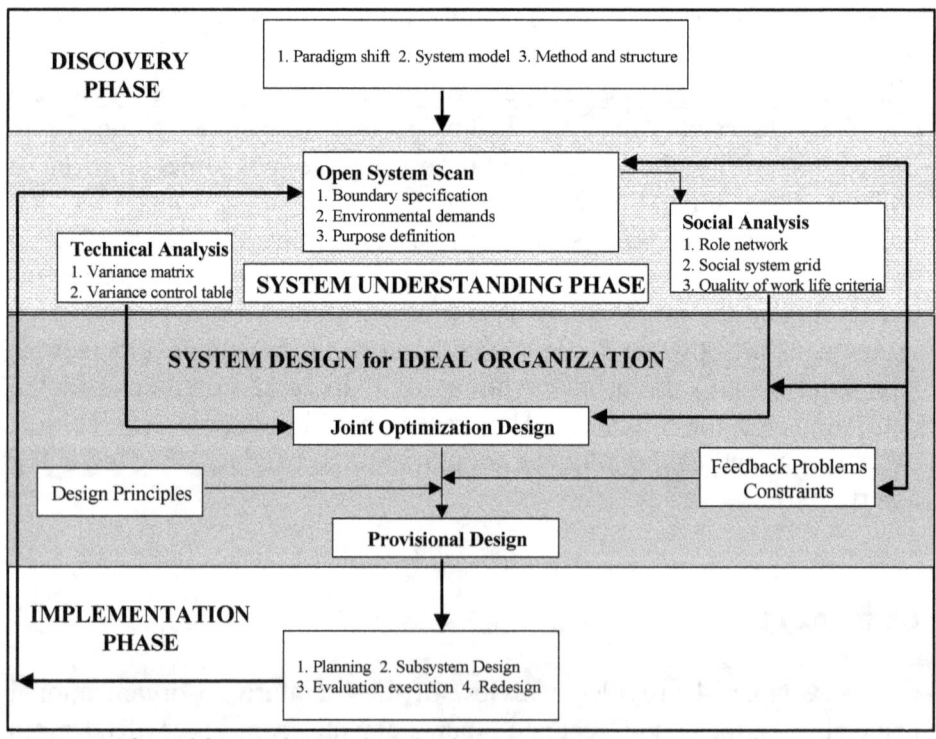

Source: *Adapted from Felton and Taylor by permission—Prentice Hall*

Figure 5-1 A Roadmap of the Phases of the STS mapped to Concert Development Process

This chapter presents an analysis of the Concert development process with respect to its compliance to the four phases of the STS model and Concert leadership styles.

The four-phase design process includes discovery, systems understanding or diagnostics (i.e., open system scan), ideal organization development, and implementation (i.e., integration of the operations). The discovery process consists of education about the STS model, project planning, and gaining management commitment. The systems understanding phase involves open system scanning of the environment—specifying organizational boundaries, creating working groups, performing social and technical analysis, consolidating data, and disseminating data to those who need them. The ideal organization development phase involves creating alternative designs, testing those designs against the organization's mission and goals, controlling key variances, contributing to quality of work life, and meeting other design criteria resulting in the creation of a provisional design. The implementation phase involves convincing all those needed for the success of the organization to participate in all aspects of strategic design, operational design/redesign, system evaluation, and continuing adjustment.

This author does not assume that he has a complete set of data to evaluate all the factors that ensure that Concert, as an organization was in full compliance with the STS design process. However, the amount of available data is substantial enough and corroborative data were obtained from multiple sources to enable good judgment.

This description involves activities performed between 1998 when the intent to form Concert was first announced and 2001 when the decision was made to dissolve the joint venture.

Concert STS Discovery Process

The discovery process involves announcing the new organization; planning the integration of socio-technical aspects of both organizations, assessing management commitment, and evaluating other start-up related issues. The process is similar to the elements in Figure 3.

In October 1998, AT&T and BT announced their plans to create a global joint venture that would combine their existing global communication partnerships to form a company that would provide global communication services to multinational corporations. Each company would contribute $5 billion U.S. dollars, either in cash or through contributions of existing assets. At the time, Concert (now called Concert Classic) was a wholly owned subsidiary of BT that had been operational and profitable for 5 years. BT donated Concert Classic to the new venture. AT&T donated its assets from World Partners, a global joint venture with some European telecommunication companies, plus some cash.

It should be noted that prior to the announcement of this GJV, BT had just divorced itself from MCI, which previously owned 25% of Concert Classic. It was a bitter divorce due to different management styles and organizational cultures. MCI's management style is conventionally American—aggressive and dynamic—while BT's style is more European and conservative. When BT announced a merger with MCI, it was "very sure" that the merger would succeed; therefore, an exit strategy was not in place (Moorhead, 1998).

Prior to obtaining approval from the Federal Communications Commission, the two organizations had begun integrating their networks. After the talks about the merger failed, substantial resources had to be expended to disconnect integrated networks. With that experience fresh in BT managers' memory, very little was done with the GJV with AT&T until BT was sure the deal would succeed. One encouraging aspect of the discovery process was the fact that management demonstrated their commitment to the venture by effectively communicating the progress of the talks on the GJV to employees of both organizations. The chairmen of both companies held all-hands meetings at several locations where the organizations had significant operations. That was one way of selling the venture to employees and discouraging them from leaving the company to join competitors.

Organizational System Understanding Process

The system-understanding process involves creating working groups and steering committees to design the new organization, developing information on the environment, identifying and analyzing the technical and social systems, gathering information, and disseminating it to various stakeholders. About 2 months after the announcement of the GJV, the AT&T/BT venture transition team was formed. The team held a 2-week workshop where a decision was made to evaluate selected Concert, AT&T, and BT systems for possible inclusion as part of the organization on the first day of its operation. The major business processes targeted for data collection from the three organizations (i.e., Concert Classic, AT&T, and BT) included service delivery, inventory database, transport network, network maintenance, customer management, customer reporting (both internal and distributor reporting), internal and distributor quality, data warehousing, and network security management. The products targeted for evaluation included network data, voice, and Internet Protocol support systems.

Organizational System Design Phase: Design for the Ideal Organization

Creating the ideal organization includes involving skilled professionals in evaluating existing Operational Support Systems (OSSs) from the three companies—AT&T, BT, and Concert; and defining the systems and architecture that would support the new company. Representatives from senior manager ranks of both companies were involved in designing the new company.

The GJV transition team named senior managers to lead the evaluation of identified OSSs and report the results of their evaluation for those functional areas where potential alternatives were identified as suitable for the new company. The presentations focused on commercially viable systems, processes, and functions that met certain basic requirements of the new company. Evaluation of the OSSs was based on information garnered from design documentation and product, service, or design reviews.

Each OSS was reviewed, based on a key set of criteria, which included functionality, scale, cost, time-scale, resources needed, and risk. A time frame and locations for the evaluations were provided. Each team was expected to provide a high-level statement of their proposed system solution within 4 weeks, and a description of each proposed system, major application, and interface within 5 weeks. Specific dates and locations of the evaluations were distributed to transition team members. AT&T members were given 5 days to meet in Red Bank, New Jersey; members of the Concert Classic team met a week later for 5 days in Reston, Virginia; and BT members met in London, England. The products evaluated include service delivery system (i.e., bid management, order management, logical network provisioning, and Internet Protocol-based network provisioning); databases for inventory management; network planning; network maintenance systems (trouble management, alarm management, network testing, and network management); customer management systems; customer reporting systems; internal/distributor reporting; systems (capacity management, and real-time performance systems); planning tools; data warehousing systems; and security management systems.

The evaluation of each product was aimed to achieve the following objectives:

1. Identify the system being proposed.
2. Understand the major functions each performs.
3. Obtain a high-level view of how the systems and processes relate to each other.
4. Assess the total range of functionality in the proposed solution.
5. Understand the full scale and cost of the development and migration required.
6. Assess the risks associated with the proposal.
7. Determine the adequacy and availability of the systems being proposed.
8. Identify the commercial relationship (i.e., intellectual property rights) in migrating the product to the GJV.

Each team was asked to describe a proposed system and its interfaces in four basic steps plus a diagram. The four steps were (a) a brief summary of functionality, (b) primary data held or passed, (c) scale (i.e., system size) and performance, and (d) current status of the system (i.e., whether it is in service or in development). OSS evaluation meetings were held and each product was judged on one of three scales: (a) not acceptable for the long term—tagged red, (b) further analysis is necessary prior to selection—tagged yellow, and (c) meets the global joint venture's long term needs—tagged green. While the technical teams focused on the technical systems, human resources personnel held parallel sessions on selecting compensation systems.

One could view the first three steps of the STS design process as part of the strategy development process. This process was well planned and documented. It appears as if the lessons learned from previous missteps had paid dividends. All that was left to do was to achieve a successful implementation process.

Implementation of Concert STS Process

The implementation process involves planning, involving people affected by the new venture, selecting recommended social and technical subsystems, integrating subsystems to form the new organization, evaluating the new organizational system, and fine tuning. The implementation phase for the new Concert began in November 1999, when the president and chief executive officer for the new organization was named. He in turn named 10 presidents, each responsible for specific functions, namely, global account, global markets, global products and services, network and systems, international carrier services, human resources, general counsel, technology leadership, chief financial officer, and communications. Each president named his/her vice presidents. International carrier services had the largest number of vice presidents (11), followed by human resources and global accounts (each with 10), and global markets with 9. This can be viewed as the beginning of the blueprint for the crooked house—Concert.

The new company, which aimed at employing 6,000 employees, opened its doors with 70 vice presidents, 10 presidents, and a chief executive officer (CEO). Starting in January 2000, each vice president named his or her directors (i.e., direct reports). The number of directors for each vice president ranged from 3 to 10. The CEO and several of the presidents and vice presidents came from other telecommunication companies, while others came from Concert Classic, AT&T, and BT. The organization chart of the new company was very traditional, contrary to what an STS model recommends. There were at least six steps from the professional staff to the president. This author used to work at the Boeing Company in Seattle, where the director of his division (operations technology unit) supervised about 3,000 employees, with only three steps from the professional staff to the director, and five steps below the company president.

The Concert directors in turn, announced their direct reports (i.e., managers) and their roles. These managers were responsible for implementing the technical and social subsystems designed by the global joint venture transition team. In January, the human resources (HR) unit extended formal offers to employees of Concert Classic, AT&T, and BT to join the new Concert. Offers were also extended to candidates outside of the three companies. In the offer letters, HR promised a Founder's bonus of 25-30 percent of each employee's salary for those who stayed with the company for 2 years. This was to discourage a "brain drain" due to the uncertainties accompanying transition, which might discourage employees. Information on employee compensation was distributed in booklets and made available at Concert's website. Other than promising a stock purchase option, the benefits offered were comparable to those from the three organizations.

The new company was registered in Bermuda and ran as a virtual organization, allowing the presidents, vice presidents, and directors to live any where in the world. For tax purposes, the new company maintained a head office in Atlanta, GA. The president for R&D for the company was also the president of R&D for AT&T. He ran the R&D operations from his office in California. Each president and vice president was required to spend one week, every month, in Bermuda with all expenses paid. It is reasonable to assume that the emphasis on tax consideration overwhelmed operational requirements, which increased operational costs and reduced the amount of time needed by the managers to devote to managing the business. The presidents and vice presidents were provided with elaborate incentives with quarterly bonuses.

Concert Leadership Model

Concert had a documented leadership policy (described later in Tables 5-1 through 5-4) that was based on path-goal theory. Path-goal theory operates on the premise that subordinates embrace a leader's behavior just as long as the subordinates view the short term or long term outcomes of the behavior as beneficial to them (Robbins, 1998). As presented by Robert House in 1971, it is the responsibility of the leader to clarify the goals of the subordinates and the paths (i.e., behaviors) that subordinates must follow to reach the goal and obtain rewards. House holds the view that clarification of the goals has positive psychological impacts on the behavior of the followers. House also claims that three moderating factors determine leadership effectiveness. These are (a) task variables—clarity of role, routine, and externally imposed control, (b) environmental contingency factors, and (c) subordinate's controllable factors (i.e., individual differences) such as personality, preferences, and expectations.

House identified four types of leadership behavior—directive leadership, supportive leadership, participative leadership, and achievement-oriented leadership. The directive leader establishes well-defined goals for the subordinates. The supportive leader is a considerate leader who is interested in the concerns of subordinates. The participative leader accepts and considers suggestions from subordinates before making decisions that affect them. The achievement-oriented leader is the type that sets goals that challenge subordinates to perform at their best. House assumes that a leader can operate in any or all of the four behavioral dimensions and in different situations.

Concert leadership model was based on four target cultures—the customer, employee collaboration, employee creativity, and results of employee's contributions to the company's strategic and near term objectives. For each target culture, the model defines three cultural and strategic leadership capabilities followed by a set of behavioral descriptors expected from the employee. This leadership model is presented in detail after the presentation of Concert performance management principles in this chapter. The leadership model is used as tool to measure employee's performance.

Concert's leadership model employed performance management principles, which was synonymous with achievement-oriented leadership behavior. It can also be called transactional leadership, which focuses on economic change to meet subordinates' current materials or psychological needs in return for contractual services. Concert defined performance management as a business activity that ensured that all employees work together to achieve Concert's business results. The following paragraphs describe Concert's performance management principles, processes, and tools. Concert measured the effectiveness of its leadership by evaluating its processes through surveys on customer interactions, employee collaboration, creativity, and results. This way, it linked individual performance with rewards. Some of the results from Concert's employee survey for the year 2000 are presented later in this chapter.

Concert Performance Management Principles

Concert defined performance management as a business activity that ensured that all employees work together to achieve Concert's business results. Its performance management principles were:

1. Create a high performance Concert team.

2. Link performance management to strategy and target culture.

3. Recognize and reward performance by (a) aligning with Concert and division-strategic priorities, (b) recognizing individual contribution to the team and to the division, and (c) rewarding both business results (i.e., what) and cultural/leadership behaviors (i.e., how).

4. Enhance performance through development by (a) encouraging continuous manager feedback and coaching, (b) encouraging manager/employee dialogue, (c) encouraging individual responsibility for development, (d) supplementing with additional assessment tools, and (e) considering multiple development approaches, not just training.

Concert promoted what it called a *life cycle* for people centered strategy implementation. The *life cycle* consists of three elements—resourcing strategy, leadership development, and rewards. To meet its resource strategy, Concert used a global resourcing strategy by recruiting across the globe, it advertised globally, and applied targeted recruiting plans. As a global telecommunication company, this strategy was important to support its customers distributed across the globe. Its people development strategy consists of a leadership development portfolio, a skill development portfolio, performance management, and succession planning. Its reward strategy includes compensation programs, ownership programs—stock purchase plans whereby employees owned a part of the company, and a benefit portfolio.

Four Phases of Concert Performance Management Activity

The four phases of Concert performance management activity were (a) objective setting to establish employee and manager's expectations, (b) mid-year review to ensure continual development, (c) annual performance review to enable employee and manager to discuss accomplishment and requirements for ongoing development, and (d) bonus award to reward employees for contributions to the company's business objectives.

Objective Setting

Between January and February of each year, the manager and employee discussed total expectations and documented key strategic objectives (What); opportunities to enhance behaviors in support of the Concert Leadership Model (How); and planned development activities using the objective setting and review form.

To establish total job expectation, the manager and employee would clarify and agree on expectations for day-to-day job performance, including any important roles, responsibilities, and requirements. To determine what the job was all about, the manager and employee had to agree on the following key strategic objectives:

1. Three to five aggressive performance objectives.
2. Manageable, achievable, direct contribution to the business.
3. Mutually agreed upon by the manager and employee.

Concert provided the employee opportunities to enhance behaviors in support of its leadership model by creating an environment where the manager and employee could discuss the leadership capabilities and associated behaviors and agree on an area of interest.

Mid-year Review: Planned Development Activities

Concert considered ensuring continual development as one of the most important aspects of performance management. The company also held the view that ongoing development could enhance individual growth and contributes to business success. To realize the greatest benefit, development planning was expected to be as specific as possible, with activities aimed to address identified employee development needs.

The company promoted multiple development approaches, not just training. The development approaches included:

- Experiential opportunities—stretched objectives that reward employees for going beyond their scope of work to help other workers or by performing special assignments, taking on project leadership, or participating in global/virtual teams
- Assessment tools—web-based career development system
- Coaching and counseling—increased manager/employee coaching discussions
- Professional coaching
- Counseling from peers and mentors
- External resources—web resources, books, articles, printed materials, and external development programs.

During the mid-year review, Concert managers and employees used the Objective Setting and Review (OSR) form created during objective setting in January/February to review progress toward goals which included: (a) progress toward key strategic objectives (What), (b) progress toward enhancing behaviors in support of Leadership Model (How), (c) progress in planned development activities, (d) how to improve results, and (e) whether it is appropriate to adjust the plan.

Annual Performance Review – December/January

Concert viewed the annual performance review as an important opportunity for the manager and employee to discuss accomplishments and ongoing development requirements. Using the same OSR form, filled out at the beginning of the year, the manager would review and discuss the following with the employee:

1. Performance against key strategic objectives (What). Summarized and discussed whether the key strategic objectives were met, greatly exceeded, or where further results/development is required.

2. Demonstrated behaviors in support of the Concert Leadership Model (How). The manager would summarize and discuss the strengths, areas meeting expectations, and areas requiring further development in the behaviors of the employee.

3. Other accomplishments.

4. Development progress and future development activities.

This was a summary of information that provided important input into Concert's Bonus Award and was used to determine salary increases during each annual salary review.

Concert Bonus Award Process

The objective of Concert's Bonus Award Plan was to reward employees for contributions toward Concert's overall business objectives. Seventy percent of the bonus award was based on company performance, while the remaining thirty percent was based on individual performance, including results of key strategic objectives and demonstrated behaviors in support of Concert Leadership Model. Concert Bonus Plan did not apply to employees that were on sales incentives or represented by a union.

Using the summary information from the annual performance review discussion, the manager would determine an overall recommendation for individual bonus percentage for award.

Concert Annual Salary Review

Concert annual salary review was driven by a number of considerations, which included market competitiveness, current salary, and the company's ability to afford the salary. One additional consideration was an employee's total job contribution, including what was achieved and how it was achieved, as determined during the annual performance review. Using information provided by the Compensation and Benefits organization and information from the annual performance review, a manager would determine an overall recommendation for individual salary adjustment.

Tabular Summaries of Concert Leadership Model

Concert leadership model targeted four cultural dimensions—the customer, collaboration, creativity, and results. These dimensions with their associated cultural and strategic leadership capabilities and behavioral descriptors are presented in Tables 5-1 through 5-4 on the pages that follow. The target culture dimensions in the first column of each table were integrated within Concert's performance management and compensation programs.

Table 5-1. Concert Leadership Model—Customer Cultural Dimension

Target Culture Dimension	Cultural and Strategic Leadership Capabilities	Behavioral Descriptors
Customer: anticipating and understanding customer global needs and placing them at the center of all we do	Customer–Centric	<ul><li>Focuses on efforts that add value to customer</li><li>Displays a commitment to anticipate and understand customer needs</li><li>Assumes ownership of customer relationship</li><li>Searches for ways to improve customer relationships</li><li>Users customer feedback to improve performance</li></ul>
	Customer/ Market Knowledge	<ul><li>Keeps up to date on business, technology, and market developments</li><li>Applies business, technology, and market knowledge to business decisions</li><li>Applies understanding of the customer to business decisions</li><li>Asks questions and encourages debate about external business environment</li><li>Recognizes opportunities for market advantage</li></ul>
	Global Effectiveness	<ul><li>Demonstrates understanding of global business management and leadership</li><li>Involves international stakeholders in business decisions</li><li>Stays informed on international trends that may impact the business</li><li>Recognizes opportunities for new business expansion across borders</li><li>Successfully establishes cross-cultural relationships; resolves potential relationship issues</li><li>Anticipates and understands potential cross-cultural communications barriers</li></ul>

Source: Adapted from Manager/Team Leader Guide, Concert Marketing, 2000

The second column of each table lists the cultural and strategic leadership capabilities to support each cultural dimension and provide the basis for leadership development. The third column identifies sample underlying behavioral descriptors for each capability. These behavioral descriptors were design for use within leadership assessments models and tools for recruitment screening.

Table 5-2. Concert Leadership Model—Collaboration

Target Culture Dimension	Cultural and Strategic Leadership Capabilities	Behavioral Descriptors
Collaboration: working effectively with each other and within and across teams, organizations, and geographic boundaries.	**Building and Managing Relationships**	<ul><li>Communicates and listens honestly and openly with no hidden agendas</li><li>Creates and maintains a network of productive long term relationships</li><li>Values and seeks the opinions of others</li><li>Empowers others with the opportunity, authority, and resources to assume accountability</li><li>Recognizes and effectively manages complex relationships and interdependencies across time, distance, organizational, and cultural boundaries</li><li>Manages conflict to strengthen relationships</li></ul>
	Company-Wide Perspective	<ul><li>Makes decisions for the good of the whole</li><li>Recognizes and leverages interdependencies to achieve business results</li><li>Removes barriers to teamwork</li></ul>
	Respect and Reward	<ul><li>Encourages individual growth and development</li><li>Celebrates successes</li><li>Shares credit with others</li><li>Coaches, encourages, and provides feedback; supports others as they learn</li></ul>

Source: Adapted from Manager/Team Leader Guide, Concert Marketing, 2000

Table 5-3. Concert Leadership Model—Creativity

Target Culture Dimension	Cultural and Strategic Leadership Capabilities	Behavioral Descriptors
Creativity: leading change and seeking innovative approaches in working relationships and business solutions	**Risk-Taking**	• Demonstrates self-awareness and self-confidence; does not fear failure • Uses the lessons of experience as opportunities to grow and learn quickly • Actively pursues new opportunities • Acts as a catalyst, initiating and leading change • Challenges existing assumptions • Considers both upside and downside of decisions and actions
	Seeking New Approaches	• Establishes directions and drives change that makes the business more effective • Encourages new ideas, supports new initiatives, and challenges traditional assumptions • Identifies new ways to achieve results • Encourages the use of technology • Demonstrates the ability to think strategically and translate change in the marketplace into business opportunity • Is flexible and readily adapts to changing environments
	Valuing Alternative Perspectives	• Seeks alternative perspectives • Encourages and values diversity within the organization • Engages and leverages diverse viewpoints • Encourages debate • Builds trust • Demonstrates sensitivity and flexibility regarding differences

Source: Adapted from Manager/Team Leader Guide, Concert Marketing, 2000

Table 5-4. Concert Leadership Model—Results

Target Culture Dimension	Cultural and Strategic Leadership Capabilities	Behavioral Descriptors
Results: delivering as promised and creating value for Concert stakeholders	**Fast, Flexible Execution**	• Is focused on results, not politics • Acts decisively/makes the call • Assumes responsibility for outcomes • Plans proactively and responds quickly to changes circumstances • Bases decisions on fact, not opinion
	Business Acumen/ Commercial Negotiation	• Understands and applies business principles toward creating competitive advantage • Understands Concert's business model and the global business context • Understands the commercial model of key market segments and where/how value is created • Approaches business relationships and interactions from a win-win perspective
	Technology/ Internet Protocol (IP) Savvy	• Holds broad, in-depth understanding of IP and its implications to Concert's and its customer's businesses • Understands IP implications for Concert's current and future customer value propositions • Integrates IP into all aspects of Concert's business • Understands and supports moving Concert capabilities up the IP value chain • Demonstrates required technical/functional content knowledge for their position

Source: Adapted from Manager/Team Leader Guide, Concert Marketing, 2000

The existence of the Concert leadership model summarized in the tables above coupled with the annual survey shows that the company had a robust leadership strategy but the failure lied in the execution of the strategy.

Concert Employee Annual Survey

In 2000, Concert conducted a company-wide survey to measure the effectiveness of the four cultural dimensions presented above. The survey was fairly short and simple with 30 core questions in six languages. Demographics were broken down by unit, region, and country and targeted the entire employee population. The survey received a response rate of 72 percent the previous year. Since the contents of the results are company confidential, the specifics of the results will not be presented in this book but some highlights that present the company in a good light, will be. Key findings of the survey showed that a majority of the respondents thought positively of Concert because they:

1. Would choose Concert again.
2. Thought their manager was flexible regarding differences.
3. Received good cooperation from peer.
4. Felt they had the freedom to do their job.
5. Would recommend Concert as a good place to work.
6. The global reach of Concert was the most valued aspect of Concert.

Concert Employee Survey core Questions

The survey asked 25 core questions with response to each question ranked on a five-value scale from Strongly Agree (5) to Strongly Disagree (0). The average score for all responses to each question ranged from 38 percent at the low end to 80 percent at the positive end. The responses to the core questions are listed below from the most favorable to the least favorable:

1. Good cooperation from unit members.
2. Manager demonstrates flexibility.
3. I have freedom to do job.
4. I trust peers in unit.
5. My unit is focused on the customer.
6. Manager supports professional growth.
7. We strive to continually improve quality.
8. Managers manage cross-cultural relationships effectively.
9. I know what is expected to achieve high performance.
10. I understand my objectives.
11. Innovative approaches are encouraged.
12. Different opinions are valued.
13. Decisions are made for the good of company.
14. We effectively use technology.
15. I have access to information.
16. I have more experience in circuit switching than in IP technology.
17. I trust senior leadership.
18. Concert is responsive to customer's needs.
19. I feel valued as an employee of Concert.
20. Senior team builds alignment.
21. Risk takers are supported.
22. Concert takes advantage of marketplace opportunities.
23. Concert communicates effectively with employees.
24. Concert's senior leaders provide clear direction.
25. Concert employees take time to have fun and celebrate success.

Concert Employee Survey Related to Concert Leadership Model—Culture Dimension

The 25 responses fell into four categories of cultural dimension—customer, collaboration, creativity, and results.

Culture dimension—customer.

The following responses received the highest scores in terms of customer relationship management:

1. My unit is focused on the customer.
2. We strive to continually improve quality.
3. Concert is responsive to customer needs.
4. Concert takes advantage of marketplace opportunities.
5. Concert's senior leaders provide clear direction.

Culture dimension—collaboration.

The following collaboration related responses received the most favorable scores with an average high of 80 percent to a low of 49 percent and an average of 64 percent:

1. There is good cooperation from unit peers.
2. Manager supports professional growth.
3. Manager manages cross-cultural relationships.
4. Decisions are made for good of company.
5. I feel valued as employee of Concert.
6. Senior team builds alignment.
7. Concert communicates effectively.

It is interesting to note that despite a daily electronic news bulletin distributed to all employees, communication still received a fairly low score in the survey. The company's organization structure was hierarchical and stove piped. This was reflected in the responses to the core culture dimension question that asked the employees to specify the quality of cooperation and teamwork received from other units of the organization. The units included: Human Resources; Global Products; Finance; Global Markets; Networks and Systems; Global Accounts; Concert Technology; and International Carrier Service units. The highest score was 35 percent while the lowest was 8 percent, with an average of 18 percent.

Culture dimension—creativity.

In terms of creativity, the following responses received the most favorable ratings from employees with the scores ranging from 51 percent to 80 percent and an average of 68 percent:

1. Manager demonstrates flexibility.
2. I have freedom to do my job.
3. I trust peers in unit.
4. Innovation is encouraged.
5. Different opinions are valued.
6. I trust unit senior leadership.
7. Risk takers are supported.

While it was true that Concert's leadership team encouraged creativity, it was encouraged just as long as it did not affect their short-term monetary returns. Research was not encouraged. The company's management was primarily interested in using off-the-shelf software to support their operations. Any creative ideas or software development effort that did not guarantee return on investment within six months was seldom funded.

Culture dimension—results.

The following responses received the most positive scores from the survey with a range of 38 percent to 73 percent, and an average of 60 percent:

1. I know what is expected to achieve high performance.
2. I understand how objectives relate.
3. Concert efficiently use technology.

4. I have access to information to do my job.
5. I can explain circuit switching versus IP technology.
6. Concert people take time to celebrate.

The fact that the highest score among the response was 73 percent is reflective of how ineffective the leadership model was. The company was performing well below expectation. The company invested heavily in building up telecommunications infrastructure, but the collapse of the technology sector prevented it from realizing anticipated income. This might have contributed to the low ratings from the employees.

Table 5-5. Open-ended Survey Questions: Valued Most and Valued Least

	Valued Most	**Valued Least**
Company	International/global reach New products /services /technologies Involved in telecommunication products/services	Poorly organized /job functions undefined Not enough resources to support products/services Lack of standardized procedures
People	Not domineering/allow employees to make decisions/ no micro-management Team oriented Diverse multi-cultural staff	Not communicative/not open; distant Not encouraging/not supportive Employee turnover too high.
Professional Opportunity	Can improve skills/learn new skills/expand my knowledge	Hard to be promoted, advancement is difficult
Compensation/ Benefits	Good benefits Good/fair compensation	Worse benefits than elsewhere Low compensation
Work Environment	Challenging Convenient location	Issues with HR department / staff Tense/too fast paced/ too much to do/ stressful Company too far flung geographically

Source: Adapted from Manager/Team Leader Guide, Concert Marketing, 2000

Responses to Open-ended Question Themes: Aspects of Company Valued Most/Valued Least

Table 5-5 above describes the responses to certain attributes of the company that were most valued and least valued by the employees. Concert's effort in conducting a survey to gauge the level of employee satisfaction is commendable, however, there was no evidence of any actions taken to address any of the employees' concerns. As stated earlier, the strategy for implementing the social aspect of the socio-technical system appears to be sound but by not using the lessons learned from employee survey as feedback mechanisms to manage the organization contributed to the failure of the joint venture.

Summary

Chapter 5 presents the application of a roadmap of the four phases of a Socio-technical System (STS) mapped to Concert development process. The four phases consist of the discovery phase or the recognition of the need for the STS paradigm; system understanding phase (i.e., open system scan, technical analysis, and social analysis); system design phase; and implementation of Concert STS phase. The chapter also describes Concert leadership model, which explains Concert performance management principles. Tables of these principles as they relate to four cultural dimensions—the customer; collaboration among employees; ensuring a creative work environment; and production of results. The chapter ends with a summary of Concert annual survey of employees to provide a view of employees' perception of the company.

CHAPTER 6: EVALUATION OF THE PROBLEMS OF CONCERT GLOBAL JOINT VENTURE AND SUGGESTED SOLUTIONS

Problems of the Joint Venture and Suggested Solutions

The research findings from this case study will support the following factors that led to the failure of Concert:

Clash of Leadership Cultures

AT&T promotes American style management, with emphasis on improving returns on shareholders' equity, while BT promotes the European management style, which focuses on extensive consultation to arrive at a consensus and pleasing the powerful labor unions possibly at the expense of shareholders' equity (Dickson, 2000).

Influences of Management Style—American versus European.

The impact of differences in management styles was evident in the new organization's operations. According to Dickson (2000), "If there is an identifiable European management style, it would tend towards extensive consultation to find out people's views before a decision is made" (p. 15). According to Jean-Paul Larçon and Bernard Ramanantsoa, professors of strategy and business policy at the HEC School of Management in Paris, the slow pace of disseminating management best practices in technical areas such as information technology and financial markets in Europe may be due to the fact "that management has to deal with people and not technical prowess. Cooperation and consultation—human issues par excellence—would appear to be two of Europe's hallmarks" (quoted in Dickson, 2000, p. 15).

Because European companies are highly unionized and management is by consensus, it takes time to make decisions and take action. This strategy worked well when the government partly or wholly owned most of the major utilities and very large organizations. Now that many of those companies have gone private, shareholders are putting pressure on managers to improve shareholders' value.

To survive these days, Dickson asserts that very large European companies must operate in a global economy. A North American management style that caters to what Dickson (2000) calls "the U.S.-driven gospel of shareholder value" (p. 15) appears to be the dominant management culture. Still, one should not overlook the merits of a people-oriented style of management, as required in STS. According to professor emeritus Philippe de Woot of the Université Catholique de Louvain, Belgium, a board member of several multinationals:

> "Europe's greatest and most original feature is diversity, but such diversity has been permeated by periods of great political or spiritual unity: the Roman Empire, the Christian Middle Ages, the Enlightenment, and contemporary European integration. These times of relative unity have left their legacy in the collective memory of Europeans. They remind us that, beyond our differences, there are also shared values and a common civilization". (Quoted in Dickson, 2000, p. 15)

Vick Luck, the managing partner for Price Waterhouse-Coopers' (PWC) management consulting practice in Europe, the Middle East, and Africa, has recognized the frustrating aspect of the European consensus-driven style of management but sees the greatest challenge as being flexible and developing the ability to translate diversity into innovation (cited in Dickson, 2000, p. 15). Larçon and Ramanantsoa view mastery of the softer issues (people issues) as the key to management success in a global economy (cited in Dickson, 2000, p. 15).

Dickson (2000) reports that Will Hutton, chief executive of the UK's Industrial Society, dismissed what Hutton calls the myth of American success and European failure with two successful European models. Hutton praised the Rhineland model, which employs sophisticated engineering-based management, dedicated to long-term investment in human resources. Hutton also noted that the German model emphasizes vocational training and demands excellence, loyalty to the company, and structured labor relations. The model has been practiced successfully for 40 years. While the Germans in Europe refuse to follow any Anglo-Saxon model, the consensus from a panel in the European Business Forum (EBF) is open to the European model. This model is characterized by cooperation, tolerance of diversity, and public interest—to the energetic influence of other systems, especially the American, which recognizes the need for competition and creation of shareholder's value in the medium term. That EBF also asserts that only those organizations that can successfully integrate the best practices from the two distinct management styles (European and American) will succeed in the global economy (cited in Dickson, 2000, p. 15). Peter Martin (2001) considers the inability of European managers to super impose their own management culture over a more sophisticated American management culture as the primary cause of merger failures.

Differences in leadership cultures--American versus European

To emphasize the differences in leadership cultures between Britons and North Americans, an article in *The Economist* titled "Why Leadership makes Britons queasy" (The Economist, October, 21, 2004) offers three possible reasons:

1. Americans have been writing about leadership longer than Britons. Over 3,000 business books are published in the United

States annually and the study of leadership forms a distinct genre in the business schools. However, the quality of many of them is hard to measure (The Economist, 12/18/2004, p.132).

2. "Britons tend not to trust charisma" (The Economist, October 21, 2004). This conjecture is attributed to long-term indoctrination in the Anglican Church where a pastor that shows too much enthusiasm in the pulpit is unlikely to be trusted. As a result, some British businessmen are more persuasive when presenting the financial health of their organization than when presenting their vision for the company.

3. To avoid being labeled as racists, American business leaders stretch themselves to make only politically correct statements in public. The Britons have a similar issue with leadership. "Leadership still awakens anxieties about class and race. Leadership was once taught on the blackboards and rugby pitches of Britain's private schools to boys who were then meant to go out to the tropics and subdue the natives" (The Economist, October 21, 2004). Such memories may still be holding back some Britons from exercising their leadership potential.

Definition of Equal Partnership—American versus European

In a so-called 50-50 partnership of the JV, the Britons were more accommodating of the more aggressive American leadership style to their own detriment. The integration of American and British (European) leadership styles was a challenge faced by Concert. The demand to meet shareholders' immediate expectations in the American system conflicts with any strategic plan to increase their return on investment over the medium term. As a result, the American style, with its emphasis on pleasing shareholders, is short sighted and can only react to uncertainties in the market place rather than being proactive in planning for an unpredictable global economy.

Absence of Trust between the Partners

The top managers from the parent organizations and Concert did not trust one another as demonstrated by the controversy over accounting reports on the value of Concert. The lack of trust came about because BT's initial value of Concert was over estimated to be $5 billion instead of $3.5 billion. The formation of a new subsidiary by BT called BT Ignite, which competed with Concert for customers, did not build any goodwill between the top managers. Hutt, Stafford, Walker, and Reingen (2000) consider trust as the most critical factor in any alliance. Trust is measured by the strength of communication links among the partners-whether they are competing instead of collaborating, and each team's integrity (i.e., honesty, opportunistic behavior, or underlying motives). All of these metrics of trust were violated through the behaviors of both partners. The JV did not appoint the Chief Executive of Concert Classic (Alfred T. Mocket) as the head of the Concert. By forming BT Ignite and making Alfred Mocket, the former head of Concert, its Chief Executive placed the *new* Concert at a huge disadvantage to compete. AT&T's decision to hire the Chief Executive of the *new* Concert, Dave Dorman, to head AT&T (replacing C. Michael Armstrong) demonstrated an opportunistic behavior that did not promote the survival of Concert.

Imbalance Structure of the New Organization

The joint venture was to be set up to operate like a new start up, without the cumbersome bureaucracies inherent in most large organizations. The fact, was that the structure of the joint venture was modeled after the parent companies with their management hierarchies and stove pipe vertical functions and minimal cross-functional interactions.

Open Competition Between Subsidiaries

Subsidiaries of the parent companies were competing for the business of the same customers with the full knowledge of the parent organizations, thereby undermining the sales of the network services of the joint venture.

Over Investment in Telecommunication Infrastructure

Expecting an economic boom, in 2000, Concert invested heavily in telecommunications infrastructure (undersea cable and fiber optics). The economic recession that followed led to excess capacity and infrastructure and large debt loads were not readily covered from revenues that could be generated with the traffic available. Concert's situation was exacerbated by the inability of Concert to retain some existing customers and to convert new customers due to the confusion reported earlier by Rendleman (2001).

Dream of Initial Public Offering

Concert's leaders were eager to issue an Initial Public Offering (IPO) for the joint venture. It had the hope of owning shares in the company, with the potential for high returns on their investments. When their dreams failed, several members of the top management left the company. The search for immediate profit motivated the leaders to set up the headquarters for the joint venture in Bermuda (off shore), with the hope of saving $1 billion from Federal tax payments during the first year alone. The leaders underestimated the cost of supporting the managers in the US and in Bermuda. As stated earlier in Chapter 5, each member of the leadership team was expected to spend one week every month in Bermuda with all expenses paid by the company. The leaders of the parent organizations, the Concert leadership team, and a large number of employees were aware of this practice. Given the cost of supporting this "tax avoidance strategy", it is difficult to determine the financial gains from such practice. It is fair to report that other companies operate off shore to take advantage of some tax loopholes in the IRS' rules; however, the implementation did not appear to be financially beneficial to Concert.

Lukewarm Embrace of Organizational Learning

The management did not embrace systems thinking and had a short-term (i.e., six months or less) view of the organization and the operations support systems. Any idea that required more than six months to start revenue generation was not funded. This may be hard to believe – but this author had first hand knowledge of this policy. As the section manager for Research and Development, it was impossible for this author to convince top Concert managers to pilot test software prototypes (developed with BT funds) that could improve the operations of the global telecommunication network with potential annual savings to the tune of hundreds of millions of dollars. Other managers reported similar experiences. Many telecommunication companies, except for the very few large corporations spend most of their "research" funds on market research. Concert managers were more interested in provisioning the network to support customer needs, buying off-the-shelf software to manage it, and improving the bottom line.

Additional Problems of the Global Joint Venture

Additional problems that were clearly evident during the operations of the joint venture but not addressed include:

- *Absence of empowerment*: Leaders imposition of their visions instead of selling shared visions.

- *Non-compliance with the tenets of STS theory*: Integration of the operations support systems from the parents did not comply with the tenets of socio-technical systems theory.

- *Absence of continuous monitoring of organizational health*: Continuous monitoring of the economic health of the joint venture was absent until it was too late for change to rescue the venture.

This case study also examined how managing the six risk dimensions could have prevented the negative impacts of the factors that caused the failure of Concert. Further this study analyzed key factors and relationships between those key factors that contributed to the demise of Concert. The data on these factors were collected from non-confidential sources, information from public sources such as, newspapers and web postings, and informal interviews of fellow employees.

Evaluation of the Operations of the Global Joint Venture from STS Perspectives

The following paragraphs identifies the areas of Concert's organization structure and operations that the leadership successfully implemented and those with disappointing results.

Successful Applications of the STS Process

In comparing Concert's organizational structure with desired characteristics for an STS-compliant model (Table 3-1) the new company was found to be strong in some areas and weak in others. The organization was strong in jointly optimizing social and technical subsystems, and employees were valued and well compensated. Individual development was encouraged depending on the disposition of the manager, and opportunities were available for employment. Employees interested in changing their jobs within the company could review several job opportunities on the company's web site and submit their resume online. Access to top management was open, and regular teleconferences were held to keep employees informed of the health of the venture. A daily electronic bulletin (The Buzz) was distributed to all employees by electronic mail to report on company operations, new markets, performance, and competitors' activities.

Weaknesses in the Implementation of the STS Process

On the down side, there were more organizational levels than recommended by the STS model. Requests for action had to travel through the organization's approval ladder. Competitive gamesmanship was common among some of the executives, who tried to build their empires instead of promoting a collaborative environment. Concert tended towards a centralized management style. This was unfortunate, because the joint venture was supposed to be managed as a startup, but its bureaucracies were just as complex as those of the parent companies. The new company, with about 6,000 employees, opened its doors with 70 vice presidents, 10 presidents, and a chief executive officer (CEO).

Starting in January 2000, each vice president named his or her directors, which ranged in number from 3 to 10 (The Buzz, 2000). There were at least **six steps** from the professional staff to the president. When this author was employed as a product design engineer at the Boeing Company in Seattle, the director of his division (Operations Technology Unit) supervised about 3,000 employees; there were only **three steps** from the professional staff to the director.

Comparison of data on Concert Leadership Model against Successful Leadership Practices

The following paragraphs describe the data collected on Concert leadership model and how they measure up against suggested successful leadership practices from the literature.

Effectiveness of Concert Leadership Model

The four culture dimensions—customer, collaboration, creativity, and results plus the responses to open-ended survey questions depicted in Table 11 provide a glimpse at the effectiveness of Concert leadership model. Comparing the responses in Table 11 against Fulmer and Wagner's (1999) best leadership practices, one could see how well Concert leadership model measured up. Fulmer and Wagner identified the eight most significant leadership practices as most significant to leadership success. These practices include leadership development and organizational change management described in the previous paragraphs. Each of the eight practices is reviewed in the paragraph below to see how Concert leadership model measured up.

1. *Alignment of leadership with organization's strategic objective is critical. To meet new business challenges, efforts must be aligned with business drivers.* Concert had a strong record on responding to

customer needs, however, the effort was not helped by competition from the subsidiaries of the parent organizations. This is a part of the customer culture dimension.

2. *Recognition of the value of human resource development and business experience—education and learning should be emphasized.* Concert provided a very good benefit and incentive program to retain employees. The company's performance could be rated as fair in the areas of education and training. While employees were encouraged to acquire additional training, education beyond the bachelor's degree level was not required nor was it encouraged.

3. *Leadership competencies should be identified and updated through internal and external training. Traits of successful leaders should be identified to drive development of leadership competencies. Once the competencies are established, they should be consistent across organizations regardless of geographic boundaries or business units.* Concert left leadership development to the initiatives of individual managers, which was inconsistent across different units of the organization. In fairness to the company, the policies were in place to follow, but compliance was not enforced.

4. *Companies are encouraged to grow their own leaders instead of recruiting from the outside.* Concert did not lock into this mindset to avoid the dangers of sticking with past successes and not looking for fresh ideas. However, the decision to replace the chief executive of Concert Classic with an outsider was one of the first missteps (in the opinion of this author) of the global joint venture.

5. *Organizations' leaders are advised to emphasize action learning. Action learning employs real time business issues to form the foundation for learning.* Concert leaders did not employ action learning. None of the company's creativity leadership behavioral descriptors included action learning.

6. *Organizations should integrate assessment, development, feedback,*

coaching and leadership succession planning. Concert's leadership model was heavy on these factors except for that of succession planning. This might have been due to the fact that some leaders were too insecure to plan for their subordinates to take their jobs or some were not motivated to step up to the next level of leadership.

7. *The human resource department should obtain support from top management level for sustaining leadership development process.* While the human resource department enjoyed support from top management, it was left to the individual managers to follow documented policies in the leadership development model for individual leadership development.

8. *Successful organizations always assess the impact of their leadership development process by using a metric to measure effectiveness.* Concert used annual employee surveys and return on investment to measure the effectiveness of the company's leadership development process.

Comparing the Concert Alliance Process against the "Seven Deadly Sins of Mergers"

Monnery and Malchione (2000) claim that more than half of all takeovers fail to create value for the buyer because the executives make certain classic mistakes. Based on their analysis of 200 recent mergers, they conclude that the most common reason for failure is underestimating the difficulty of successful post merger integration (PMI). Angus Knowles-Cutler and Rob Bradbury (2002) came to the same conclusion in their review of Deloitte and Touche study of mergers and acquisitions; so did Moorhead (1998). They identify seven of those classic mistakes.

In the following paragraphs, I will review Concert's global joint venture in light of these seven 'deadly mistakes' plus one—poor attention to customer needs. It should be noted that Concert was a joint venture and not a merger, but the same factors should apply.

1. *Missing Strategic Opportunities. Managers should realize that strategic opportunities are not limited to cost savings.* Cost saving was not touted in the Concert deal. Instead, synergy and both companies' ability to benefit from each other's global success (AT&T in North America and BT in Europe) were stressed.

2. *Managing Change Without Leading. Merely having focus groups, newsletters, and teleconferences does not replace leadership and giving directions to staff.* Concert's performance in this area can be considered adequate. It took three to six months, between the announcement of the merger and selection of the full management team. The differences between the two management styles and conflicting issues among organizational units were left unresolved for too long.

3. *Expecting to realize most benefits by the end of the first year.* Concert fell into this trap. Their expectation of realizing $7 billion in revenue and $1 billion in profits by the end of the first year was overly ambitious. Concert did not achieve this goal, which was one of the reasons for the establishment of the company's headquarters off shore in Bermuda. The profit for Concert Classic (the old Concert) could not be determined because it was operated as a wholly owned subsidiary of BT without a separate line item for its profits. However, the expected profit figures for the new Concert was based on Concert Classic's performance. After initial missteps in Concert valuation, AT&T finally contributed $3.5 billion worth assets to the new company. The $10 billion company then became a $7 billion company.

4. *Assuming equal treatment for all partners.* This contributed to the downfall of Concert. Someone has to be in charge. In a 50-50 partnership, it is difficult to resolve deadlocks. In Skapinker's

view, "Mergers of equals can be so dangerous because it is not clear who is in charge" (FT, April 12, 2000). On reporting on the merger of Nextel and Sprint in December 11 issue of the *Washington Post*, White and McCarthy (2004) stated that the language that called the deal "merger of equals" was included to treat the deal as a tax-free transaction, which is never enforced. The use of a transition team to evaluate and recommend specific business models at the beginning of the joint venture was effective in establishing good working relationships among participants. One could compare this situation with a marriage. Somebody has to be responsible to have the final say on specific issues without which the marriage would not work. As much as the parent companies claimed that they backed Concert 100 percent, the actions of their respective sales force going after the same customers did not support their claim.

5. *Using a one-size-fits-all approach for each business unit— funding each business unit at the same resource level regardless of their location.* It is generally suggested that local environments should be used to determine resource allocation. In the absence of knowledge about resource allocation within Concert, this author cannot offer any comments on this issue.

6. *Managers believing that they cannot stabilize the organization until all the facts are known.* Stability was critical to retaining existing customers and employees. It was important to let employees know that their jobs were safe; otherwise, valuable employees might have left. The promise of founders' bonus for employees who stayed for the first two years provided a stable work force. However, the differences between the two styles of leadership (American and European) influenced performance of the employees. This point is discussed further in the Risk Management section.

7. *Declaring victory prematurely and failing to track changes that are promised.* The transition team was disbanded too early. The

team needed to stay in place to monitor the implementation process and track the benefits being realized. At that time most members of the transition team belonged to the new company. Given the stove pipe structure of the organization, it was important to have had a service release management team with the authority to oversee the end-to-end design and delivery of telecommunication services to the customer and to coordinate the activities of several vertical organizations. A team called the Solutions Design Team was formed later in April 2001 and disbanded in December of 2001. It would have been more beneficial to Concert had the team been formed sooner. The team would have been able to identify the gaps in communication between the stove-pipe business units and improve organizational performance.

Table 6-1. Report of the University of Michigan Study on American Customer (Post Merger) Satisfaction Index

Buyer	Target	Change in Customer Satisfaction		Company Response
		Customer	Buyer	
Charter Comms.	AT&T Broadband Assets	-12.7%	-4.7%	Does its best to satisfy customers
Qwest	US West	-12.5%	-1.4%	Dramatically improved its service last year
BP	Amoco	-8.4%	-3.8%	Company survey reports a higher customer satisfaction
First Union	Core States	-8.1%	-2.8%	Paid high premium and consolidated operations too quickly
SBC	Ameritech	-7%	-4.1%	Company survey reports improved quality of service
Dillard's	Mercantile Stores	-6.8%	0%	Declined to comment
Exxon	Mobil	-6.3	-3.8	Company survey did not support negative customer satisfaction
Bank One	First Chicago	-5.7%	-2.8%	Delayed integration of operations
WorldCom	MCI	-5.4%	-4%	Almost every carrier had a merger that affected customer service
J.C. Penney	Eckerd	-3.8%	-1.4%	Diverted focus from fixing department stores; failed to dominate drug retailing
AT&T	Telecommunications	-2.7%	-4.1%	Declined to comment; sold the assets
Kroger	Fred Meyer	-2.7%	0%	Success overall; understand must satisfy customer every time they shop
Unilever	BestFoods	-2.4%	-2.4%	Declined to comment
Kraft	Nabisco	-1.2%	-1.2%	Declined comment
First Union	Wachovia	+10.6%	+5.6%	Focused on retaining customers and took more time to integrate
Nestlé	Ralston Purina	+3.7%	+1.2%	Quickly introduced new and improved product
Bell Atlantic	NYNEX	+1.4%	-3.9%	Bell Atlantic took advantage of the best practices and people
General Mills	Pillsbury	+1.2%	-1.2%	Quickly extended PR push for Pillsbury lines

Source: Reported by Business Week (12/6/2004); Data provided by the University of Michigan & Thomson Financial

The challenges of integrating business processes from two companies

Integrating business processes from two companies is a very difficult task (Monnery & Malchione, 2000). The benefits promised to the stakeholder cannot be realized unless the seven traps described above are avoided.

This author would add the eighth deadly sin: *Not considering the impact of customer reaction to the merger*. In a study sponsored by *Business Week* and conducted by the University of Michigan and Thomson Financial Corporation on American Customer Satisfaction Index found that 50% of consumers report that they are less satisfied two years after a merger. "It can take years for companies to change customers' feelings and stop any losses" (Emily Thornton, *Business Week*, December 6, 2004, pp. 58-63). A statistical summary of their findings depicted in Table 6-1 shows that, 14 out of 18 high-profile mergers left consumers, the acquiring company and the industry unsatisfied two years after the merger.

Additional reports show that the change in average customer satisfaction index two years after merger by industry is not encouraging—Gasoline (-7.4%); Cable (-6.4%); Retail (-5.3%); Telecoms (-3.7%); Banks (-0.8%); Food (+0.9%). (Thornton, 2004, page 63).

Validation of Data on Causes of the Failure of the Joint Venture

The following paragraphs describe the use of data source and investigator triangulation protocols to validate the findings of this case study.

Data Source Triangulation

Jamil Khan (2001) an employee of Concert wrote a report on *The Decline of Telecomms Industry with Special Reference to Concert*. Khan was one of the employees that this author interviewed for this study. Khan collected his data from the same sources from which this author obtained his data. These data include information on Concert networks, Concert management, BT and AT&T organizations, and the causes of failure of the company.

Investigator Triangulation

The causes of failure as reported in Khan's (2001) report were compared with the factors that were identified earlier as the causes of failure in this study. Khan identified the following factors for failure Concert's failure:

1. Prevailing business climate—technology bust
2. Competition
3. Internet convergence
4. Single global network model
5. Conflicts between AT&T and BT and their legacy of monopoly
6. Flaws in the business plan
7. Management structure
8. Cultural clashes.

Prevailing Business Climate—Technology Bust

Khan (2001) noted that the chief executives of AT&T and BT blamed the economic climate for the failure of Concert. Sir Peter Bonfield, the chief executive of BT, claimed that the demise of Concert was inevitable given the downturn in the telecomm sector. "Since Concert was conceived as an international venture the global marketplace in our sector has changed out of all recognition and we need to change with it" (http://www.cio.com, December, 2001).

C. Michael Armstrong, AT&T chairman and chief executive, blamed the failure of Concert on the market and shrinking profits and not the ability of the two companies to get along. "There was never an issue with compatibility. We just didn't get the results we wanted" as reported in (http://www.cio.com). These claims contradict the Deloitte and Touche study (Knowles-Cutler & Bradbury, 2002). Since the formation of the joint venture, both companies' stocks took severe beatings (BT from $245 to $40, AT&T from $65 to $14 per share). In addition, BT Ignite, a wholly owned subsidiary of BT, had lost more revenue that the joint venture. It was just convenient to blame external forces for the failures. When the merger was announced in 1998, BT's market capitalization was $115 billion and AT&T was valued at about $140 billion. Therefore at that time the parent organizations valued Concert at less than 10 percent of each parent's market value. The parent companies contributed less than 5 percent of their market value to form Concert. Appendix B contains information on the profiles of AT&T and BT showing company management and their effectiveness, and other statistics. It also shows that after selling off some of their divisions, BT had a market capitalization of $32.8 billion while AT&T was valued at $52.8 billion.

Competition.

Sales representatives from the parent organizations and from their wholly owned subsidiaries competed for the same customers. Sales representatives sold incompatible products to the same customers. The companies had different agendas that prevented them from agreeing on a single strategy.

Internet Convergence.

The Internet had lowered the barrier to access to the Internet/Telecom market. Companies could then use the Internet for both their data and voice communication service needs and obtain their services from several Internet Service Providers (ISPs). In the UK a company could become an ISP with a startup cost of $120,000 (Telephony Online, December 2001). In most markets, including Europe and North America these ISPs did not and still do not have to deal with regulatory hurdles that the Telecom Service Providers (TSPs) must confront because their services are seen as value-added services. Concert was set up as a small company to compete with the ISPs. In fact, it developed a product called Virtual ISP (VISP) but due to internal conflicts (www.concert.com, 2001) between Concert and BT, it was not able to win enough contracts. In addition, it sold its services through a third party distributor in Australia (Sharinga).

A Single Global Network Model.

Concert's model of being a single telecommunication service provider for multi-national companies (MNCs), otherwise known as one-stop-shopping for all their voice and data communication needs, had the benefit of providing a consistent service through out the world where the MNC had its offices. This model failed because, while Concert had control over its global core network, it had to deal with local regulation in each country and had to rely on local or regional network distributors. It did not have any control over some of the distributors who were responsible for providing the services to the end customers. Therefore, it could not guarantee delivery of communication service to its customers, yet it was penalized for poor service delivery. This is also one of the major reasons for the failure of the company. A better business model would have been to develop layered networks where Concert owned and managed the core networks and controlled access to the customers. The company was investigating this business model, which WorldCom was using when the parents announced the closure of the joint venture. This is an example where the competition (WorldCom), which bought MCI communications, saw a flaw in Concert's business model and developed their own to render Concert's model ineffective. Concert also lost business because many MNCs were worried about putting all their eggs in one basket. They dealt with several providers for better pricing and reliability (http://www.cio.com).

Conflicts between AT&T and BT and Monopolies Legacy.

The alliances were formed primarily to protect territories that were threatened by the 1996 Telecommunications Act that deregulated telecommunication services. BT saw the joint venture as an opportunity to gain more business clients in the US, while AT&T saw it as the chance to establish a solid presence in Europe. The parent companies found themselves competing with Concert in both markets. To address this issue, BT formed a wholly owned subsidiary called BT Ignite to compete against Concert and AT&T in Europe. AT&T had originally planned to merge its global network-Advanced Global Network Service (AGNS), a business that it bought from IBM with Concert, but it changed its mind because of BT's move.

Prior to the formation of the new Concert, Alfred T. Mocket, the head of Concert Classic had promised to help the new Concert establish a strong presence in Europe (with the expectation that he would be named to head the new Concert). When he was not selected, he convinced BT to form BT Ignite and he was selected to head it. BT Ignite did not view Concert as a partner, instead, Concert was viewed as a competitor and was treated as such. BT Ignite did not help AT&T establish itself in Europe as previously expected.

GlobalOne, another global joint venture between Deutsche TeleKOM, France Telecom, and Sprint also collapsed due to a similar situation. The parent companies found themselves competing in the same territory as their offspring (i.e., their subsidiaries).

Flaws in the Business Plan.

After the announcement to close the company the president of Concert and his direct reports admitted that Concert's business model was flawed. They agreed that the business model of going through distributors to sell Concert network services, without the ability to control service level agreements was flawed. Secondly, they acknowledged that the cost of integrating the networks of both parents was higher than expected. Thirdly, while most of the customers were based in the US and most telephone calls originated from the US, AT&T was burdened with paying a larger number of distributors overseas to deliver calls to its customers. AT&T had to pay more than BT even though this was supposed to be a 50-50 partnership. This was because the contract between the two parents mandated that the owner of the network where the calls originated was responsible for the calls and the circuits.

Management Structures.

As described in the Concert Implementation Process section, Concert's organizational structure was organized as stove pipe business units with minimal cross-functional communications. The business units included global accounts, global services, concert technologies, information technology, and engineering. This structure made integration of business services that required contributions from several units difficult to achieve.

Cultural Clashes.

Aside from different leadership styles between the British and Americans (Dickson, 2000), and those presented at the beginning of this chapter, there were significant differences in the working methods. Khan (2001) claims that the British and Europeans tend to be more generalists and discuss things a lot and in more details before proceeding to the project information phase. Americans were found to be more specialized and more concerned with deliverables, deadlines, and the bottom line.

The Importance of Communication and Cultural Understanding Between Partners

In this author's view, Peter Martin (2001) gives one of the most compelling culture-oriented-reason on why European management fails in American business management environments. He asserts:

> "American management culture is extremely powerful. It is included in the country's excellent business schools, and reinforced by a business publishing industry that endlessly recycles the values and principles of the best companies. This makes it very difficult for overseas acquirers to superimpose their own culture". (Peter Martin, Financial Times, June 2, 2001).

While there is some truth to the assertion, Jennifer Merritt (2004) warns about some problems in educating future leaders. Even in the best US business schools they are just beginning to teach lasting principles of leadership including business ethics. According to her in depth report on the top US and International business schools, the challenges of teaching leadership in the best business schools to students who already view themselves as leaders is daunting (Merritt, 2004; pp.63-90). . In the same issue of *Business Week* in an article titled "Is the Focus Too Fine?" Diana Middleton (2004) reports on how many of the programs stress only marketable skills at the expense of sound core curriculums.

In her article titled the "Power of Talk, Who gets heard", Tannen (1995) provides a discerning analysis on the influence of one's linguistic style on conversations and how it affects human relationships, especially in organizational settings. "We all know what confidence, competence, and authority sound like," Tannen says. "Or do we?" (p. 138). She is convinced that "communication isn't as simple as saying what you mean" (p. 138). She claims what is crucial is how one says what one means, which varies from one individual to the next because how one uses language is a learned social behavior. One's cultural experience has significant influence on how one talks and listens. Tannen (1995) claims that people are judged by the way they present themselves, which is commonly through talk. The style of speaking one learned as a child determines whether one is perceived as competent or confident and affects who gets heard, who gets the credit, and the level of work performed.

English versus English—Separated by a Common Language (Winston Churchill)

While one assumes that the British and the Americans speak English, the difference in the cultures and communication styles is much wider than most people assume. Appendix A is provided to help the reader get a better understanding of how the two nations (UK and US) are *divided by a common language*. Appendix A provides tables that describe the differences in languages as used within the British and the US cultural, business, transportation, etc. environments. In addition to helping both cultures to understand each other, this author hopes that Appendix A will clarify the confusion faced by those of us who studied under both systems and need to communicate effectively within both cultures. Joint ventures are bound to fail unless the leaders are aware of the significance of the cultural differences and their impacts on building relationships. While there are many benefits to joint ventures, Hutt, M. D., Stafford, E. R., Walker, B. A., & Reingen, P. H. (2000) attribute the failure of many alliances to inattention to personal relationships between the employees of the partnerships.

Evaluating the Collapse of Concert from a Risk Management Perspective

While investigator triangulation was used in the previous paragraphs to validate the results of this study, the six risk dimensions, proposed by Moorhead (1998), were used for methodological triangulation. This approach provides better insights into why Concert failed as an organization by identifying specific theoretical assumptions that were violated. These risk assumptions involve: *complexity of the organizations being merged* (low or high); *dynamic complexity of the industry* (stable or turbulent); *compatibility of the partners' cultures* (common or divergent profiles); *partner compatibility as to trust* (strong or weak mutual trust); *alignment of goals and principles between partners* (compatible or divergent); *alignment dynamics in handling conflicts* (collaborative or adversarial).

Risk Dimension #1: Structural Complexity of Concert (low or high)

The complexity of the merged company can be low, moderate, or high. Concert was a complex organization because it had several business units and multiple layers of managers. It also had several products and services with interdependent operations, strategy, and capital planning. The pace of the merger was rapid (about one year). As a complex system, its social and technical elements should have been managed as living systems to ensure survival. Since Concert was not managed as a complex adaptive system, it did not survive.

Risk Dimension #2: Dynamic Complexity of Industry (stable or turbulent)

Concert was in the telecommunication sector, a turbulent industry where the business environment changes continuously. The industry was evolving rapidly. To survive Concert had to launch new products, new ways of managing them, and new competitors who were entering the industry on a regular basis with changing strategic intents. This dynamic complexity made the business a high-risk operation that needed to be managed as a complex adaptive system. Again Concert did not address this risk effectively.

Risk Dimension #3: Partner Compatibility—corporate cultures (common or divergent profile)

Concert culture was a hybrid of the parent organizations' cultures because most of the employees came from the parent organizations. This created a laboratory to practice the European style of leadership with interest in extended discussions and consensus building prior to decision-making. The same laboratory had American style of management wed to the bottom line mindset and employees were viewed as tools to get the job done. Such a divergent profile required rigorous planning and coordinated strategies, local autonomy, and end-to-end view of process design, development and service delivery.

A review of Mitchell Marks and Philip Mirvis (1998) Merging Cultures Evaluation Index (MCEI) with nine culture-oriented variables can be used to understand the important roles that cultures play in mergers and acquisitions of companies from different cultures. The value of each variable ranges from one to five from least desirable to most desirable. The variables are:

1. Role/Process orientation versus results orientation.
2. Concentrated power versus diffused power.
3. Horizontal influence versus vertical influence.
4. Innovation versus tradition.
5. Wide flow of information versus narrow flow of information.
6. Problem solving (i.e., thinking versus acting).
7. Rewards versus recognition.
8. Decision-making: consensus, consultative, or authoritative.

9. Attributes of valued employees recognized: values, skills, or results.

MCEI can be used to understand corporate cultures to enhance partner compatibility. Marks and Mirvis observed that, organizations with cultures that do not fully mesh to allow for some learning by both sides, are bound to fail. The rapid pace of integration activities at Concert did not allow enough time for the cultures to mesh and organizational learning to take root.

Risk Dimension #4: Partner Compatibility (strong or weak mutual trust)

Mutual trust between the partners was weak. While the two partners respected each other's competence and integrity, they were skeptical about each other's openness, dealing in good faith, and predictability. As described earlier, BT formed BT Ignite to compete with Concert. Such a move did not engender trust between the partners.

Risk Dimension #5: Alignment of Goals and Principles (compatible or divergent)

As explained in the legacy of monopoly above, the partner organizations were out to protect their interests to insulate themselves from the effects of deregulation. The partners did not see the expected benefits of the joint venture as balanced or fair, and therefore commitment to the joint venture was not equal. AT&T did not gain access to European distributors as expected while most of Concert's operations were located in the US.

Risk Dimension #6: Alignment Dynamics – Handling Alliance Conflict (Collaborative or Adversarial)

Conflicts are easier to handle when there is a 51 percent control, that way someone is in charge. It is difficult in a 50-50 relationship. Most managers are, to the extent possible, open to new ways of doing business. Many managers limit their attention to measurable factors that they can control, such as the number and size of new customers, time to market for new products, and return on investments (ROI). A significant number of managers at Concert ignored those hard to measure soft variables such as trust, motivation, commitment, creativity, risk-taking, leadership, credibility, relationship building and repair, values, attitudes, and openness to cross-cultural learning. There was a need to develop ROI measures for these soft variables because they needed to be managed for any joint venture to succeed. The failure of Concert can be attributed in part to poor management of the six risk areas outlined above.

Summary

Chapter 6 provides some insights into the causes of the collapse of the global joint venture. The causes include clash of cultures, conflicts in the styles of management—American versus European; absence of trust between the partners; imbalance organizational structure (top-heavy); and half-hearted support for organizational learning. The chapter also compares the data on Concert leadership model against successful leadership practices from the literature. The operation of the alliance was evaluated in the light of the so-called "seven deadly sins" of mergers and acquisitions. A table of American Consumer Satisfaction Index regarding mergers supports previous research that most mergers and acquisitions do not benefit the customers, the buyer, and the industry. Validation of data on the causes of the failure of the joint venture using data source and investigation protocols was also presented. The joint venture was also evaluated from a risk management perspective defined by six risk assumptions: (a) structural complexity of the organization, (b) dynamic complexity of the industry; (c) compatibility of the cultures of the partners; (d) partner compatibility as to trust; (e) alignment of goals, principles, and dynamics in handling conflicts; and (f) the leadership ability to manage risks in the six risk areas.

CHAPTER 7: CONCLUSION

In this case study, I have presented, analyzed, and evaluated the factors that caused the failure of Concert, a $10 billion global joint venture between AT&T and BT. Most of the factors that led to failure of the company have been critically analyzed. The analysis corroborates the evidence reported by other researchers and practitioners on the alarming failure rates of mergers and acquisitions with a significant drain on the economy. One significant factor is poor integration of the systems of the partners, otherwise known as the implementation process. This implementation process includes managing the new organization with a constant focus on strategic goals, building new and better organization, attending to the human element, and building a desired organizational culture (Marks & Mirvis, 1998).

I have reviewed Concert's organization from a socio-technical system perspective. While the design of the technical aspects of the organization was commendable, the implementation of the plan was flawed. This is reported by several authors to be typical of many joint ventures. The development of Concert fits into the typical failure scenario whereby the leaders of the partners negotiate the partnership, announce it, and sign the contract leaving the implementation to the managers from different cultural and organizational cultures that must work together. These managers devote most of their efforts to measurable and what they consider as tangible factors at the expense of soft variables such as relationship building and conflict resolution, which if not addressed can destroy the venture the same way that measurable factors can. These soft variables and integration issues needed to have been addressed by Concert and other failed alliances to reduce the high failure rates of joint ventures.

Over $100 billion worth of mergers and acquisitions were consummated during the last quarter of 2004. In addition to the $41 billion merger of Cingular Wireless LLC and AT&T Wireless Inc. in October 2004, the *Network World* issue of December 20, 2004 included a report titled "Merger Mania Mounts" with a list of companies with mergers and acquisitions to the tune of $59 billion during the fourth quarter of 2004. The mergers include Symantec and Veritas ($13.5 billion), Sprint and Nextel ($35 billion), Oracle and PeopleSoft ($10.3 billion), K-Mart and Sears and several others. The December 6, 2004 issue of *Washington Post* also reported on the acquisition of the London-based British firm of DLA LLP by Piper Rudnick Gray Cary LLP of Washington DC. The merger calls for the integration of 2,700 lawyers in 18 countries (Washington Post, 12/6/2004, pp. E1-E2). Another transatlantic merger of BAE Systems PLC of Great Britain with the US-based United Defense Industries Inc., the maker of the Bradley Fighting Vehicles for $4.2 billion is a very good case to watch.

Hopefully, the leaders of these newly merged organizations can learn from the findings of this case study and reduce the number of possible crooked houses on the corporate landscape.

REFERENCES

Beer, M., & Eisentat, R. A. (2000). The silent killers of strategy implementation and learning. Sloan Management Review, 41(4), 29-40.

Beinhocker, E. D. (1999). Robust adaptive strategies. Sloan Management Review, 40(3), 95-109.

Birnberg, J. G. (1998). Some reflections on the evolution of organizational control. Behavioral Research in Accounting, 1998 Supplement, 10, 27-46.

Brynjolfsson, E., & Renshaw, A. A. (1997). The matrix of change. Sloan Management Review, 38(2). 37-54.

Busby, J. S. (1999). The effectiveness of collective retrospection as a mechanism of organizational learning. Journal of Applied Behavioral Science, 35(1), 109-130.

Carroll, J. S., & Hatakenaka, S. (2001). Driving organizational change in the midst of crisis. MIT Sloan Management Review, 42(3), 70-79.

Collins, J. (2001). Good to great: Whay some companies make the leap and others don't, HarperCollins Publishers Inc., New York, NY.

Concert. (1999). Human Resources Initiative. http://insiteremote.concert.com/humanresources/hrint.asp.

Creswell, J. W. (1998). Qualitative inquiry and research design: Choosing among five traditions. Thousand Oaks, CA: Sage Publications.

Creswell, J. W. (1994). Research design: Quantitative & qualitative approaches. Thousand Oaks, CA: Sage Publications.

Dickson, T. (2000). A model of cooperation. Financial Times: Management—European Business (adapted from European Business Forum, 1, 2000), April 13.

Dent, E. B., & Goldberg, S. G., (1999). Challenging "resistance to change." Journal of Applied Behavioral Science, 35(1), 25-41.

Duke, D. L. (1998). The normative context of organizational leadership. Educational Administration Quarterly, 34(2). 165-195.

Etzioni, A. (1975). A comparative analysis of complex organizations: On power, involvement and their correlates. The Free Press, New York.

Flood, R. L., & Carson, E. R. (1993). Dealing with complexity: An introduction to the theory and application of systems science. Second Edition, Plenum Press, New York.

Fox, W. M. (1995). Socio-technical system principles and guidelines: Past and present. Journal of Applied Behavioral Science, 31(1), 91-105.

Fulmer, R. M., & Wagner, S. (1999). Leadership: Lessons from the best. Training and Development, 53(3), 28-34.

Gregersen, H. B., Morrison, A. J., & Black, J. S. (1998). Developing leaders for the global frontiers. Sloan Management Review, 40(1), 21-31.

Grinblatt, M, & Titman, S. (2002). Financial markets and corporate strategies, (2nd Edition) New York, McGraw-Hill, Irwin.

References

Harari, O. (1999). Why do leaders avoid change? Management Review, 88(3). 35-39.

Hax, A. C. & Wilde II, D. L. (1999). The delta model: Adaptive management for a changing world. Sloan Management Review, 40(2), 11-28.

Hofstede, G. (1997). Cultures and organizations: Software of the mind—intercultural cooperation and its importance for survival. New York: McGraw-Hill.

Hutt, M. D., Stafford, E. R., Walker, B. A., & Reingen, P. H. (2000). Case study: Defining the social network of a strategic alliance. Sloan Management Review, Winter, 51-62.

Isaac, S, & Michael, W. B. (1989). Handbook in research and evaluation: For education and the behavioral sciences (2nd ed.). San Diego, CA: EDITS Publishers.

Kenney, R. A., & Schwartz-Kenney, B. M. (1996). Implicit leadership theories: Defining leaders described as worthy of influence. Personality & Social Psychology Bulletin, 22(11), 1128-1143.

Khan, J. (2001). The decline of the telecomms industry with special reference to Concert. Concert Global Networks, LLC, Reston VA. 15 pp.

Kirchmeyer, C. (1998). Determinants of managerial career success: Evidence and explanation of male/female differences. Journal of Management, 24(6), 673-692.

Knowles-Cutler, A., & Bradbury, R. (2002). Viewpoint: Why mergers are not for amateurs—a new professional body of specialists would help stop a vicious circle of failing deals. Financial Times, February 12, 2002, London, UK, p. 12.

Malone, T. W., Crowston, K., Lee, J., Pentland, B., Dellarocas, C., Wyner, G., Quimby, J., Osborn, C. S., Bernstein, A., Herman, G., Klein, M. & O'Donnell, E. (1999). Tools for inventing organizations: Toward a handbook of organizational processes. Management Science, 45(3), 425-443.

Malone, T. W. (1997, Winter). Is empowerment just a fad? Control, decision making, and IT. Sloan Management Review, 23-35.

Marks, M. L., & Mirvis, P. H. (1998). Joining Forces: Making One Plus One Equal Three in Mergers, Acquisitions, and Alliances. San Francisco, Jossey-Bass Publishers.

Martin, P. (2001). Shoals across the pond: Why do so many acquisitive European companies flounder in the US? Financial Times-Personal Finance, June 2, 2001.

McNally, J. A., & Gerras, S. J. (1996). Teaching leadership at the U. S. Military Academy at West Point. Journal of Applied Behavioral Science, 32(2), 175-188.

Merritt, J. (2004). The best B-Schools: Exclusive rankings of the top U.S. and International MBA programs. Business Week. October 18, 2004, 63-76, 90.

Monnery, N., & Malchione, R. (2000, February 29). Seven deadly sins of mergers. Financial Times-Management Viewpoint, p. 16.

Moorhead, D. (1998). Reflecting on the BT-MCI Merger. Slide Pack, BT Group, North America, Reston, VA.

Moorhead, D. (1998a). Risk management for partnerships, alliances. Slide Pack, Organizational Research, BT Group, North America, Reston, VA.

References

Moorhead, D. (1996). MCI/BT/Concert/Avantel Alliance/ Venture Review Conference: Summary of lessons learnt: Recommendations to BT Management. 19 Nov. 1996.

Odubiyi, J., Bayless, G. & Ruberton, E. (2001). Victor – Proactive fault tracking and resolution in broadband networks using collaborative intelligent agents. In A. L. G. Hayzelden & J. Bigham (Eds.), <u>Agent technology for communications infrastructure</u> (chapter 20). London: John Wiley and Sons, Ltd.

O'Hara, M. T., Watson, R. T., & Kava, C. B. (1999). Managing the three levels of change. <u>Information Systems Management, 16</u>(5), 63-70.

Pascale, R. T. (1999). Surfing the edge of chaos. <u>Sloan Management Review, 40</u>(3), 83-94.

Pitts, R. A., & Lei, D. (1997). Building cooperative advantage: Managing strategic alliances to promote organizational learning. <u>Journal of World Business, 32</u>(3), 203-224.

Popper, M., & Lipshitz, R. (1998). Organizational learning mechanisms: A structural and cultural approach to organizational learning. <u>Journal of Applied Behavioral Science, 34</u>(2), 161-180.

Rendleman, J. (2001). AT&T and BT: Concert's out of tune with the times. Duo dissolves disappointing $10 billion global telecom venture. Informationweek.com, Oct. 26, p. 26.

Reuters (2002). Welch says rivals to benefit from HP deal. <u>In Brief/Technology. http://www.latimes.com/business/la-000009770feb08.story</u>? Los Angeles Times.

Rockart, J. F., Earl, M. J., & Ross, J. W. (1996). Eight imperatives for the IT organization. <u>Sloan Management Review,</u> Fall 1996, 43-55.

Roth, G., & Kleiner, A. (1998). Developing organizational memory through learning histories. Organizational Dynamics, 27(2), 43-60.

Schein, E. H. (1996). Three cultures of management: The key to organizational learning. Sloan Management Review, 38(1), 9-21.

Schriesheim, C. A. (1997). Substitutes-for-leadership theory: Development and basic concepts. Leadership Quarterly, 8(2), 103-109.

Scott, W. R. (1998). Organizations: Rational, natural and open systems. Englewood Cliffs, NJ: Prentice Hall.

Senge, P. M. (1990). The leaders new work: Building learning organizations. Sloan Management Review, 1-17.

Skapinker, M. (2000). Marrying in haste. Comment & Analysis. Financial Times, April 12, 2000.

Smith, A. W. (1997). Leadership is a living system: Learning leaders and organizations. Human Systems Management, 16(4), 277-286.

Stake, R. (1995). The art of case study research. Thousand Oaks, CA: Sage Publications.

Stebbins, M. W., & Shani, A. B. (1998, February). Organization design and the knowledge worker. The Journal of Systemic Knowledge Management, 1-12.

Taylor, J. C., & Felten, D. F. (1993). Performance by design: Socio-technical systems in North America. Englewood Cliffs, NJ: Prentice-Hall.

References

Tannen, D. (1995). The power of talk: Who gets heard and why. Harvard Business Review, 73(5), 138-148.

Tetenbaum, J. (1998). Shifting paradigms: From Newton to chaos. Organizational Dynamics. Spring98. (26)4, 21-32.

Thornton, E. (2004). Why consumers hate mergers: Business Week. December 5, 2004. 58-63.

White, B. & McCarthy, E. (2004). Next, Sprint close to merger. Washington Post. December 11, 2004. A1, A8.

APPENDIX A. CULTURAL ISSUES: TWO NATIONS (UK AND US) DIVIDED BY A COMMON LANGUAGE

The following tables (adapted from Concert (Classic) Instructional Broadcast, 1994) describe the differences in languages as used within the British and American (primarily US) cultural environments—business related, accommodation, buildings, jobs, household, transportation, clothes and things, food and things, expressions, and spellings.

A1: Business Related

English (US)	English (UK)
Mail	Post
Resume	Curriculum Vitae (CV)
Call	Ring
Information	Directory enquiries
Oxymoron	Contradiction
Eraser	Rubber
The plan	The way forward
To table	To put to one side
To put on the agenda	To table
Semester	Term
File	Folder
Notebook	File
Foils	Acetates/overheads
Tent cards	Name plates
Name tag	Name badge
Stocks	Government bonds
Trillion	Billion
White out	Liquid paper /sno-pake /tippex
Block	Tranche
8 ½ " X 11"	A4 (Standard paper size)
Custom built	Bespoke

English (US)	English (UK)
Slate	List of candidates
CEO/SVP	Director/Senior Manager
Streamline	Rationalise
Rationalize	Make excuses for
Ginn	Order
2/4/02	4/2/02 (4th Feb 02)
4/2/02	2/4/02 (2nd Apr 02)
Schedule	Diary
Calendar	Diary
Schedule	Timetable
Money	Dosh
Check	Cheque
Bill	Note

A2. Accommodation/Buildings/Jobs

English (US)	English (UK)
Apartment house	Block of flats
Apartment	Flat (rented)
Condominium	Private flat
Duplex	Semi
1st floor	Ground floor
2nd floor	1st floor
Bar	Pub
Diner	Cafe
Theater	Cinema
Store	Shop
Mall	Shopping centre
Elevator	Lift
Secretary	Typist
Personal assistant	Secretary
Sheriff	Chief Constable
Garbage collector	Dust man or Dustbin man
Mail	Char/cleaner

Appendix A: Two Nations Divided by a Common Language

A3. Household etc.

English (US)	English (UK)
Facilities	Domestics
Maid	Domestic/cleaner
Vacuum cleaner/Vacuum cleaning	Hoover/Hoovering
Restroom/bathroom	Toilet/loo
The John	Toilet
Bar owner	Publican
Liquor store	Off licence
Private school	Public school
Public school	Private school
Telephone booth	Telephone box/kiosk
Doctor's office	Surgery
Cot	Single bed
Crib	Cot
Hoarding	Bill board
Subdivision	Estate
Room mate	Flat mate
Small writing desk	Davenport
Davenport	Sofa
Faucet	Tap
Sod	Turf
Yard	Back Garden
Deck	Balcony
Wrench	Spanner

A4. Transportation/Getting around

English (US)	English (UK)
Sedan	Saloon
Rental car	Hire car
Soft top	Convertible
Truck	Lorry

English (US)	English (UK)
Lamp	Light
Blinkers	Indicators
Muffler	Exhaust Pipe
Trunk	Boot
Hood	Bonnet
Windshield	Windscreen
License plate	Number plate
Transmission	Gear box
Stick shift	Gear stick
Strut	Shock absorber
Track	Tread
Gas	Petrol
Parking lot	Car park
Interstate	Motorway
Beltway	Ring Road
Rest area	Lay by
Traffic signal	Traffic light
Median	Central reservation
Traffic circle	Roundabout
Yield	Give way
Honk	Beep
Baggage claim	Baggage reclaim
Exit	Way out
Freight train	Goods train
Trolley/street car	Tram
Tram	Cable car
Railroad	Railway

A5. Clothes & Things

English (US)	English (UK)
Comforter	Duvet
Shopping Cart	Shopping Troley
Buggy	Push chair
Baby carriage	Pram
Garbage/trash	Rubbish
Pot holder	Oven glove
Flashlight	Torch
Sneakers/walkers	Trainers
Tennis shoes	Pumps
Pumps	Court shoes/high heels
Jumper	Pinafore
Sweater	Jumper
Undershirt	Vest
Vest	Waistcoat
Underpants	Knickers
Pants	Trousers
Zipper	Zip
Nylons/tights	Support stockings
Panty hose	Tights

A6. Food and Things

English (US)	English (UK)
Appetizer	Starter
Entrée	Main course
Napkin	Serviette
Osterizer	Liquidiser/blender
Over easy	Lightly fried upside down egg
Over medium	Medium fried upside down egg
Over well	Well down fried egg
Rot	Go off

English (US)	English (UK)
Garbage/trash	Rubbish
Filbert	Hazelnut
Biscuit	Scone
Cookie	Biscuit
Muffin	Bun
Candy	Sweets
Candy bar	Chocolate bar
Raisin bread	Tea cake
Chips	Crisps
French fries	Chips
Jalapenos	Chilies
Mamoza	Bucks Fizz
Zucchini	Courgette
Squash	Marrow
Pots	Pans
Flatware	Baking trays
Hot pot	Kettle
Pitcher	Jug
Broil	Grill

A7. Expressions

English (US)	English (UK)
Hey	Hello
Thanks	Cheers
Sorry? What did you say?	Pardon?
Excuse me	Sorry/Pardon me
Quite	Very
Fairly	Quite
Figure out	Suss out
Know what I'm saying	See what I mean
Uh huh	You're welcome
Exhausted	Knackered
Broken	Knackered
Napping	Kipping
Very pleased	Chuffed

Appendix A: Two Nations Divided by a Common Language

English (US)	English (UK)
Very poor	Naf
Fixin'	Getting ready to
Cool	Very smart/good
Neat	Great
Cute	Pretty
Work out	Suss out
Goof off	Skive off
Darn	Damn
Slam dunk	Dead certain
Ham	Show off
Dweeb	Idiot
Goober	Idiot
Hickey	Idiot
Hickey	Love bite
Bangs	Fringe
Hem haw	Indecisive/procrastinate
Bomb	Dismal failure
Great success	Bomb
Flaky	Cracked/eccentric
Give a flak	Give a stick
Exclamation point	Exclamation mark
Period	Full stop

A8. The Spellings

English (US)	English (UK)
Tire	Tyre
Check	Cheque
Center	Centre
Color	Colour
Harbor	Harbour
Program	Programme
Vise	Vice
Behavior	Behaviour
Targeted	Targetted

A9. Pronunciations (or Pronounciations)

Tomato
Buoy
Stalactite
Process

A10. Use of Zee (or Zed), etc.

English (US)	English (UK)
Organize	Organise
Rationalize	Rationalise
Generalize	Generalise
Recognize	Recognise
Exclamation point	Exclmation mark
Period	Full stop

APPENDIX B. PROFILES AND HISTORICAL SHARE PRICES OF AT&T, BT, AND MCI

The information on company profiles and historical data are available from http://finance.yahoo.com. The interested reader can obtain fairly comprehensive information on each company by entering appropriate stock symbols (T for AT&T, BTY for BT and MCI for MCI) and selecting menus for profiles, charts, etc. In November 2005 the FCC approved the acquisition of **AT&T Corp.** by **SBC Communications Inc.** for roughly $16 billion in cash and stock. The new company will retain the AT&T's name. The FCC also approved the merger of Verizon Communications with MCI.

APPENDIX C. LIST OF ACRONYMS

AGNS	Advanced Global Network Service (a business unit of
ATM	Asynchronous Transfer Mode
AT&T	American Telephone & Telegraph
BT	British Telecom
BTplc	British Telecommunications private limited company
CEO	Chief Executive Officer
CIO	Chief Information Officer
CST	Contingency Systems Theory
EBITDA	Earning Before Interest, Tax, Depreciation, and Amortization
GJV	Global Joint Venture
GMP	Global Managed Platform
IPLC	International Private Line Circuits
IPO	Initial Public Offering
ISP	Internet Service Provider
IT	Information Technology
MCEI	Merging Cultures Evaluation Index
MNC	Multi-National Companies/Corporations
OSS	Operational Support System
PLC	Private Limited Company
PMI	Post Merger Integration
PWC	Price Waterhouse-Coopers
ROI	Return On Investment
STS	Socio-Technical System
TMF	TeleManagement Forum
TMN	Telecommunication Management Network
TOM	Telecom Operations Map
VISP	Virtual ISP

INDEX

Page numbers followed by f indicate figures. Page numbers followed by t indicate tables. Page numbers followed by n indicate notes.

A

achievement-oriented leadership, 70
acquisitions. *See* mergers and acquisitions
action learning, 59, 96
action research, 32, 38
Advanced Global Network Service (AGNS), 106
aerospace industry mergers, 13
alpha change, 43, 44t
American Customer Satisfaction Index, 101t, 102
American Telephone & Telegraph Inc. *See* AT&T
Ameritech, 101t
Amoco, 41, 101t
And complex organizations, 26
Armstrong, C. M., 90, 104
Arthur Andersen (firm), 52–53
asynchronous transfer mode (ATM) switches, 10
AT&T. *See also* Concert Global Networks Inc.
    acquisition of Tele-Communications, 101t
    Advanced Global Network Service, 106
    conflicts with BT, 106
    contribution to Concert, 64, 98
    management style, 86
    market capitalization, 104
    motivation for Concert venture, 106
    Operational Support System evaluation, 65–67
    and overseas distributors, 107, 112
    stock price before and after Concert, 104
AT&T Broadband Assets, 101t
AT&T Wireless Inc., 115–16
axiological assumption, 22t

B

Bank One, 101t

BAE Systems PLC, 116
Beer, M., 47, 57, 58
Beinhocker, E. D., 47
Bell Atlantic, 101t
Bermuda, as headquarters location, 69, 91–92, 98
beta change, 43, 44t
Birnberg, J. G., 27, 27t, 28, 29, 29t
Black, J. S., 47, 53
Boeing Company, 68, 95
Bonfield, P., 103–4
BP, 41, 101t
Bradbury, R., 3, 41, 46, 48, 51, 97, 104
British Telecommunications. *See* BT
British Telecom North America (BTNA), 4
BT. *See also* Concert Global Networks Inc.
    action learning, 59
    background, 13–14
    conflicts with AT&T, 106
    contribution to Concert, 64, 90
    failed merger with MCI, 14–15, 64–65
    management style, 86
    market capitalization, 104
    motivation for Concert venture, 106
    Operational Support System evaluation, 65–67
    payments to overseas distributors, 107
    stock price before and after Concert, 18–19, 104
BT Ignite, 90, 104, 106, 112
business climate, 104
business management layer, 11, 12f
business savvy, 53
business unit funding, 99
Business Week, 101t, 102, 108
Buzz, The, 94, 95

C

Carroll, J. S., 47, 56, 57
Carson, E. R., 31, 32
case study research, 3–4, 23–26
cell 1 organizations, 27, 27t, 29t

Index

cell 2 organizations, 27, 27t, 29t
cell 3 organizations, 27–28, 27t, 29t
cell 4 organizations, 27t, 28, 29t. *See also* non-routine organizations
centralization, 45–46, 45t
change, 42–44, 44t, 54–58, 98, 99–100
charisma, mistrust of, 89
Charter Comms., 101t
Chief Information Officers (CIOs), 60
Cingular Wireless LLC, 115–16
CIOs (Chief Information Officers), 60
collaboration, 42, 77t, 82–83
communication, 64–65, 108–9
company failures, 41
Compaq Computer Corporation, 18
competition between subsidiaries, 91, 104
complex organizations, 28, 29t, 30
compliance theory, 33–34
Computer Sciences Corporation, 7
Concert Classic
    background, 13–14, 13n
    chief executive, 90, 96, 106
    and Concert Global Networks, 64
    MCI ownership of, 64
    Operational Support System evaluation, 65–67
    profit, 98
    transition team, 65
Concert Global Networks Inc. *See also* AT&T; BT
    accounting controversy, 90, 98
    annual performance review, 74
    annual salary review, 75
    background, 9–11, 9f, 12f
    bonus award process, 74–75
    business model flaws, 1, 107
    collaboration cultural dimension, 77t, 82–83
    communication with employees, 64–65
    competition between subsidiaries, 91, 104
    cost of, 1, 3–4, 9, 64
    creativity cultural dimension, 78t, 83
    cultural clashes, 107–8

cultural dimensions, 70, 76t–79t
customer cultural dimension, 76t, 82
data source triangulation, 103
discovery process, 64–65
dissolving of, 7
and economic climate, 103–4
employee annual survey, 80–85, 84t
employee compensation, 68–69, 69, 99
employee education and training, 94
employee objective setting, 72–73
employee values, 84t, 85
empowerment, 93
failure of, 1-2, 3, 102–9
founder's bonus, 68, 99
global managed platform, 9–10, 9f
global network model, 105–6
goals, 16
implementation phase, 67–69
Initial Public Offering dream, 91–92
integration process, 3
and Internet convergence, 105
investigator triangulation, 103–8
language differences, 109
leadership cultures, 86–89
leadership development, 71, 96
leadership model, 69–70, 75–76, 76t–79t, 79–80, 95–102, 101t
leadership succession planning, 96–97
life cycle for strategy implementation, 71–72
management structures, 107
mid-year review, 73
mistrust between partners, 90
as non-routine organization, 26, 28, 30
organizational development process, 62–85
organizational health monitoring, 93
organizational learning, 92
performance management principles, 70–75
personnel, 67–68, 94–95
resource strategy, 71
results cultural dimension, 79t, 83–84

reward strategy, 71–72
risk management perspective, 110–13
second-order change, 44
socio-technical systems perspectives, 93–94
Solutions Design Team, 100
subsystems, 30
system design phase, 65–67
system understanding process, 65
telecommunication infrastructure, 91
transition team, 65, 99–100
valuation of, 90, 98, 104
Virtual ISP (VISP) product, 105
contingency systems theory, 32
Core States, 101t
Creswell, J. W., 3, 21, 22t, 23, 23t, 24, 25, 60
cultural aspects of study, 26
cultural clashes, 107–8, 108–9
cultural dimensions, 76t–79t
cultures
    leadership, 86–89
    management, 50–51

D

data source triangulation, 61
decentralization, 45–46, 45t
decision information, and empowerment, 45–46, 45t
Decline of Telecomms Industry with Special Reference to Concert, The (Khan), 103
Dell Inc., 18
Deloitte & Touche, 41, 42, 48, 97, 104
Dent, E. B., 47, 54
Denzin, N., 60
Deutsche TeleKOM, 106
development process, 5–6
Dickson, T., 47, 86, 87, 107
Dillard's, 101t
directive leadership, 69–70
discovery process, 64–65
diversifications, profitability of, 6

DLA LLP, 116
Dorman, D., 90
duality of purpose, 53
Duke, D. L., 46, 48, 49

E
Earl, M. J., 47, 60
EBF (European Business Forum), 88
Eckerd, 101t
economic climate, 103–4
Economist, The, 89
Einstein, A., 54
Eisentat, R. A., 47, 57, 58
element management layer, 11, 12f
Elgin, B., 18
emotional connection, 53
employee participation in change, 56–57
empowerment, 45–46, 45t
engineers' culture, 50
epistemological assumption, 22t
Etzioni, A., 34
European Business Forum (EBF), 88
executives' culture, 50–51
external adaptation, 49–50
Exxon, 101t

F
Favaro, K., 4
Felten, D. F., 31, 33, 62, 62f
Financial Times, 17
Fiorina, C., 18
First Chicago, 101t
first-order change, 43, 44t
First Union, 101t
Flood, R. L., 31, 32
Ford Aerospace, 13
Fox, W. M., 35, 37, 38, 39t
France Telecom, 106
Fred Meyer, 101t

Fulmer, R. M., 47, 58, 95
funding, business unit, 99

G
gamma change, 43, 44t. *See also* socio-technical systems theory (STS)
GE, 18, 52
GE Institute, 52
General Mills, 101t
German model of management, 88
Gerras, S. J., 46–47, 51
global network model, 105–6
GlobalOne, 106
Goldberg, S. G., 47, 54
government contracts, 51
Gregersen, H. B., 47, 53
Grinblatt, M., 3, 6

H
Harari, O., 3, 47, 54–55, 56
Hatakenaka, S., 47, 56, 57
Hewlett-Packard, 18
Honeywell, 18
House, R., 69
human relations model of the organization, 31
Hutt, M. D., 17, 42, 46, 90, 109
Hutton, W., 88

I
IBM, 106
implementation phase, 67–69
implicit leadership theory, 48
Information Technology departments, 60
integrity, 53
interaction leadership theorists, 49
internal integration, 49–50
Internet convergence, 105
investigator triangulation, 61
Isaac, S., 23–24
"Is the Focus Too Fine?" (Middleton), 108

J
J.C.Penney, 101t
Joining Forces (Marks and Mirvis), 3–4
joint ventures. *See also* Concert Global Networks Inc.
    benefits to, 17
    failures, 1, 3–4, 17
    versus mergers and acquisitions, 5–6
    reasons for, 5
    risk dimensions, 7

K
Kava, C. B., 42, 43, 44t
Kenney, R. A., 46, 48
Khan, J., 103, 107–8
Kirchmeyer, C., 47
K-Mart, 116
Knowles-Cutler, A., 3, 41, 46, 48, 51, 97, 104
Kraft, 101t
Kroger, 101t

L
Larçon, J.-P., 86, 87
leadership
    characteristics, 53–54
    cultures, 86–89
    development, 46–47, 51–54
    effectiveness, 69
    global, 53–54
    normative view of, 48–49
    and organizational change, 47, 54–58
    perspectives, 46, 48–51
    practices, 47, 58–59
    and promotion from within, 58–59, 96
    types, 69–70
learning organizations, 48
LePlay, F., 24
life cycle for strategy implementation, 71–72
localization, 53–54

Lockheed Martin Aerospace, 13
Loral Aerospace, 13
Los Angeles Times, 18
Luck, V., 87

M
Malchione, R., 97, 103
Malone, T. W., 45, 45t, 46, 50
management cultures, 50–51
　American *versus* European, 47, 86–88, 108–9
management structures, 107
Manager/Team Leader Guide, 76t–79t, 84t
Marks, M. L., 3–4, 7, 111, 112, 115
Martin, P., 3, 17, 47, 88, 108
McCarthy, E., 3, 99
MCEI (Merging Cultures Evaluation Index), 111–12
MCI, 13–14, 18, 65, 101t
McNally, J. A., 46–47, 51
Mercantile Stores, 101t
"Merger Mania Mounts," 116
mergers and acquisitions
　in aerospace industry, 13
　customer reaction to, 101t, 102
　failure rate, 4, 6–7, 16, 17–18
　failure reasons, 17–18, 97–102, 101t, 115
　versus joint ventures, 5–6
　losses *versus* profits, 1, 6
　money invested in, 4, 19, 115–16
　reasons for, 5
　risk dimensions, 7
　shareholder returns, 5
　successful, 4–5, 4n
Merging Cultures Evaluation Index (MCEI), 111–12
Merritt, J., 108
methodological assumption, 22t
methodological triangulation, 61
Michael, W. B., 23–24
Middleton, D., 108
military, leadership development in, 51–52

Milosevic, S., 48
Mirvis, P. H., 3–4, 7, 111, 112, 115
MITRE Corporation, 52
Mobil, 101t
Mocket, A. T., 90, 106
Monnery, N., 97, 102
monopolies legacy, 106
Moorhead, D., 3, 6–7, 14–16, 18, 46, 59, 64, 97, 110
Morrison, A. J., 47, 53
motivation, and empowerment, 45–46, 45t
multi-national companies, and telecommunication service providers, 105–6

N
Nabisco, 101t
Nestlé, 101t
network management layer, 11, 12f
Network World, 116
Nextel, 3, 99, 116
non-routine organizations, 26, 28, 29t, 30. *See also* cell 4 organizations
normative view of organizational leadership, 48–49
NYNEX, 101t

O
Odubiyi, J., 9f
O'Hara, M. T., 42, 43, 44t
ontological assumption, 22t
Operational Support Systems (OSS) evaluation, 65–67
operators' culture, 50
Oracle, 116
organizational change, 42–43, 44t, 54–58, 98, 99–100
organizational control, 29–30, 29t
organizations
    and change management, 44t
    as complex and open systems, 26–28, 27t
    human relations model, 31
    learning, 48
    non-routine, 26, 28, 29t, 30
    purposeful *versus* purposive, 33
    rational model, 31

social perspective, 37
  as socio-technical systems, 33–34, 35f
  systems model, 31–32
  technical perspective, 36–37
  technical system *versus* technology, 42
  traditional model *versus* socio-technical systems theory, 39t
organization theory, branches of, 31–32
OSS (Operational Support Systems) evaluation, 65–67

P
Palumbo, S., 19
paradigm selection, 21, 22t, 23t
participative leadership, 69–70
partners
  absence of trust between, 90
  collaboration among, 42
  communication and cultural understanding between, 108–9
  compatibility of, 111–12
  equal treatment of, 89, 98–99
path-goal theory, 57–58, 69
PeopleSoft, 116
Piaget, J., 24
Pillsbury, 101t
Pinochet, A., 48
Piper Rudnick Gray Cary LLP, 116
points of presence (PoP), 9
power, and resistance to change, 55
"Power of Talk" (Tannen), 108–9
Price, C., 17
project managers, and change management, 44t
project team, and change management, 44t

Q
qualitative paradigm, 21, 22t, 23t
quantitative paradigm, 22t
Qwest, 101t

R
racism, anxiety about, 89

Ralston Purina, 101t
Ramanantsoa, B., 86, 87
rational model of the organization, 31
Reingen, P. H., 17, 42, 46, 90, 109
Rendleman, J., 19, 91
Reuters, 18
rhetorical assumption, 22t
Rhineland model of management, 88
Rockart, J. F., 47, 60
Ross, J. W., 47, 60

S
Santayana, G., 2
SBC, 101t
Schein, E. H., 3, 46, 49, 50, 51
Schriesheim, C. A., 46, 51
Schwartz-Kenney, B. M., 46, 48
Scott, W. R., 31, 32, 33
Sears, 116
second-order change, 43, 44, 44t
Senge, P., 48
service management layer, 11, 12f
Shani, A. B., 26, 30, 62
shareholder returns, 5
Sharinga, 105
Shell Corporation, 53
Simon, H., 49
Sirower, M., 17
Skapinker, M., 3, 4, 17, 18, 98–99
Smith, A. W., 46, 48
socio-technical systems
    background, 31–32
    designing, 38
    organizations as, 33–34, 35f
socio-technical systems theory (STS), 31–40
    design process overview, 62–63, 62f
    development of, 32–33
    discovery process, 64–65
    implementation phase, 63, 67–69, 115

managing levels of organizational change with, 42–43
　　　principles of, 33–34
　　　social perspective of the organization, 37
　　　system design phase, 63, 65–67
　　　system-understanding process, 63, 65
　　　technical perspective of the organization, 36–37
　　　versus traditional model of organizations, 39t
soft variables, 41, 50, 87–88, 113, 115
Sprint, 3, 99, 106, 116
stability, lack of, 99
Stafford, E. R., 17, 42, 46, 90, 109
Stake, R., 23, 24, 25, 60, 61
Stebbins, M. W., 26, 30, 62
strategic opportunities, missed, 98
strategy, in successful mergers, 4n
strategy implementation life cycle, 71–72
STS. *See* socio-technical systems theory (STS)
study
　　　abstract of, 1-2
　　　assumptions, 21, 22t
　　　conclusions, 115–16
　　　cultural aspects, 26
　　　motivations for, 17–19
　　　purpose, 19
　　　significance, 19
　　　as single case study, 25–26
　　　triangulation protocols for validating results, 60–61, 61
subsidiaries, competition between, 91, 104
substitutes-for-leadership, 51
supportive leadership, 69–70
Symantec, 116
system design phase, 65–67
systems model of the organization, 31–32
system-understanding process, 65

T
Tannen, D., 108–9
Tavistock Institute of Human Relations, 32–33
Taylor, J. C., 31, 33, 62, 62f

technical system, 42–43
technology, 42–43, 51
technology bust, 103–4
Telecommunication Management Network (TMN) model, 10–11
Telecommunications Act (U.S.), 13, 106
Tele-Communications (firm), 101t
Telecom Operations' Map (TOM), 10–11, 12f
TeleManagement Forum (TMF), 10, 12f
theory triangulation, 61
third-order change, 43, 44t. *See also* socio-technical systems theory (STS)
Thomson Financial Corporation, 101t, 102
Thornton, E., 5, 18, 102
Titman, S., 3, 6
TMF (TeleManagement Forum), 10, 12f
TMN (Telecommunication Management Network) model, 10–11
TOM (Telecom Operations' Map), 10–11, 12f
traditional model *versus* socio-technical systems theory, 39t
transactional leadership, 49, 70
transformational leadership, 49
triangulation, 60–61, 103 89, 103–8
trust, 45–46, 45t, 90, 112

U
Unilever, 101t
United Defense Industries Inc., 116
University of Chicago, Department of Sociology, 24
University of Michigan, 101t, 102
US West, 101t

V
Veritas, 116
Virtual ISP (VISP) product, 105

W
Wachovia, 101t
Wagner, S., 48, 58, 95
Walker, B. A., 17, 42, 46, 90, 109
Walter. J. R., 54
Washington Post, 99, 116

Watson, R. T., 42, 43, 44t
Weber, M., 31
Welch, J., 18
White, B., 3, 99
"Why Leadership Makes Britons Queasy," 88–89
"Why Mergers Are Not for Amateurs" (Knowles-Cutler and Bradbury), 41
Woot, P. de, 87
World Bank, 53
WorldCom, 14, 18, 101t, 105–6
World Partners, 64
Wright, O., 21

ABOUT THE AUTHOR

Jidé B. Odubiyi, Ph.D., is the President and Chief Technology Officer of SEGMA LLC, a technology development and consulting firm in Silver Spring, MD. He serves as a research consultant on intelligent systems engineering and distributed computing for the Advanced Architectures and Automation Branch of NASA Goddard Space Flight Center in Greenbelt, MD. He is a Technology Advisor to Owen Software Development Corporation (Rockville, MD), a software technology company focused on creating Adaptive Decision Support solutions for education and career planning. Prior to his current position, he served as associate professor of computer science at Bowie State University in the University System of Maryland where he taught graduate and undergraduate courses in Artificial Intelligence (AI), Computer/Network Security, and Computer Programming Languages. He also served as the director of the Laboratory for Information and Infrastructure Security and Assurance (LIISA), a laboratory that he established with funding from the National Science Foundation and equipment donation from Cisco Systems Inc. His research and writing focus on computer and network management and security, intelligent agent technology, distributed computing, and leadership and organizational change management.

This book is a product of the author's scholarly research and experience as a Principal AI Researcher and R&D Manager at British Telecom North America/Concert Global Communications (USA) in Reston, VA. For over five years he was responsible for leading and directing research projects focused on development of speech recognition systems, agent technology, application of distributed intelligent agents to network management, and intelligent search engines. He holds B.S. degrees in both Mechanical and Industrial Engineering and an M.S. degree in Mechanical Engineering from the University of Washington, and a Ph.D. degree in Applied Management and Decision Sciences from Walden University. He also holds a Ph.D. degree in Computer Science. He has 25+ years of experience in developing large decision support systems for different organizations including the Boeing Company in Seattle, WA; Lockheed Martin Aerospace in Seabrook MD, and The MITRE Corporation in McLean, VA.

Index